D1492303

000091754

PAUL GAYLER
VIRTUALLY Vegetarian

Lucinda Rogers

Paul Gayler

Virtually Vegetarian

With a Foreword by Anton Mosimann

Imaginative Vegetarian Recipes, with Meat, Poultry and Fish Variations

HarperCollins*Publishers*

Dedication

To my wife Anita, who encourages, nurtures and supports me every day of my life.
To my parents, Lilian and Stan, for their love, support and guidance during the early part of my career.
To my first teacher, Alf Rounce, and to Remy Fougère and Anton Mosimann, who
between them instilled a love of good food in my heart.

Acknowledgements

I gratefully acknowledge the assistance of the following people, without whom
this book would not have been possible:
all at HarperCollins, for their help and encouragement.
Jane Suthering, food stylist, and Jane Middleton, editor, whose help and guidance have been invaluable;
I deeply value their support, friendship and professionalism.
My fruit and vegetable suppliers, Danny and Bett Murphy of Chefs Connection, for their generosity and
co-operation in supplying beautiful produce for me to work with.
My sous chefs Chris Galvin, Julian Marshall, Selwyn Stoby, Tony Moyse and James Holland, whose
help and daily dedication to fine food made this book possible.
Miguel Frascione, for his assistance with the wine notes.
Fiona Lindsay, my agent, for her tireless help and friendship.

First published in 1995 by
HarperCollins*Publishers* London
Reprinted 1995

Text © Paul Gayler 1995
Photographs © Andrew Whittuck 1995
All rights reserved

Paul Gayler asserts the moral right to be identified as
the author of this work

EDITOR: *Jane Middleton*
TEXT DESIGNER: *Joan Curtis*
PHOTOGRAPHER: *Andrew Whittuck*
HOME ECONOMIST: *Jane Suthering*
STYLIST: *Sue Russell*
ILLUSTRATOR: *Lucinda Rogers*
INDEXER: *Susan Bosanko*

For HarperCollins Publishers
COMMISSIONING EDITOR: *Polly Powell*
PROJECT EDITOR: *Barbara Dixon*
DESIGN MANAGER: *Caroline Hill*

A catalogue record for this book is available
from the British Library

ISBN 0 00 412737 4

Typeset in Galliard
Colour reproduction in Singapore by Colourscan
Printed and bound in Italy by LEGO Spa

FRONT COVER: Swiss Chard and Date Ravioloni with Roasted Peppers, page 78

*F*oreword

When Paul Gayler told me that his first book, *Virtually Vegetarian*, was to be published, I was delighted for him.

We first met in 1979 at the Mouton Cadet Menu Competition lunch, at which I was a guest. Paul won that award and, a year later, came to work as my Sous Chef at The Dorchester. During the following two years, he was often on my team at culinary events throughout Europe. Now a friend and respected colleague, Paul has become one of the leading chefs in the country.

Paul shares my passion for cooking and, in particular, has always demonstrated his love and respect for vegetarian food: his dishes are beautifully presented, well balanced, and full of flavour. The influences of his travels around the world are evident in the inspired way he uses spices and seasonings – some oriental, some Mediterranean and some Middle Eastern. His creative palette is wide.

The recipes in this book also show that Paul has his finger on the pulse of today's eating trends. I know from my own clientele that there are a great number of people who, while not strictly vegetarian, enjoy the occasional meat-free meal. They aren't purist about their vegetarian food – they eat it because they enjoy it, feel healthier for it, and relish the exciting new taste sensations a good chef can bring to such dishes. Paul has for a long time recognised what these customers want – his vegetarian menus were among the first to be seen – and he has now firmly established his reputation as an innovative champion of Haute Cuisine Végétarienne.

But he doesn't ever forget that you should never impose your tastes on others, so his suggestions here for adapting some of the recipes to suit those whose tastes are still meaty will be extremely useful to readers. I was pleased to see the wine notes as well, since the question of what to drink with the frequently stronger flavours of vegetarian food can be perplexing.

Like me, Paul is an avid collector of cookery books. *Virtually Vegetarian* is assured a place on my shelves; it is a book which anyone who loves food, vegetarian or not, will want to own.

Anton Mosimann

Contents

Introduction

My interest in vegetarian cuisine began in 1984, quite by chance, when I read an article by a leading vegetarian food writer complaining that one of London's top hotels had been unable to provide him with anything more exciting for lunch than a nut cutlet. At the time I was working as chef director at Inigo Jones in London's Covent Garden, and I decided to try offering a vegetarian option. I devised a seven-course vegetarian menu, christening it the Menu Potager (garden menu). It quickly won friends and excited media interest, although some were rather baffled about my intentions. Looking back, I suppose it was quite revolutionary for its time. Vegetarian cooking had not been taken seriously in top restaurants before and had certainly not been raised to the status of *haute cuisine*. I saw vegetarianism not only as an exciting new way of eating but also as a challenge for my chefs, an opportunity for them to extend their repertoire. A year later I was asked to present a television programme on vegetables and vegetarian food for the 'Take Six Cooks' series.

Since then, interest in vegetarian food has grown so dramatically that it is now impossible to ignore. The days when there was a bleak choice between tofu and lentils or cheese salads and omelettes are over and, in an effort to woo a new clientele, top chefs are combining exotic ingredients with staple foods to create imaginative new dishes and flavour combinations.

Initially my vegetarian menu relied on classic French techniques – the backbone of good cooking – to create sophisticated meatless dishes. Gradually, though, I began to incorporate oriental and Middle Eastern influences which opened up a whole new range of flavours. Similarly, over the past few years the Mediterranean/Californian influence has had a profound impact on vegetarian food and encouraged everyone to break away from the 'meat-and-two-veg' pattern. The revolution in our eating habits has been abetted by an influx of new foods – supermarkets and delis now stock ingredients that were undreamt of only a few years ago.

What is strange, perhaps, is that despite the escalating interest in vegetarianism there has not been a parallel increase in the number of vegetarian restaurants. It appears that the most delicious vegetarian food springs from the kitchens of meat-eating cooks. During my 20 years as a chef, some of the best vegetable dishes I have eaten around the world have been the creations not of vegetarians but of all-round cooks who love good food.

Many people have made a conscious effort to change their lifestyle over the last decade and this has meant changing the way they eat. Hopefully the days of fad diets are over, and we now look for longer-term solutions to the challenge of staying healthy. Vegetarianism can offer an easy route to good health. However, I would be the last person to join the crusade for a nutritionally correct but indulgence-free diet. Take a look at the recipes in this book and you will see impeccably healthy dishes, consisting of little more than fresh vegetables and olive oil, side by side with more lavish creations that rely on butter, cream and cheese. Vegetarianism does not have to equal puritanism, and in my view eating should be a pleasure, not a duty.

In the 1990s, as vegetarianism moves increasingly into the mainstream, a new phenomenon has emerged – that of the 'virtual vegetarian'. This is the term I have coined for people who eat vegetarian food most of the time simply because they enjoy it. With the rich gastronomic choice now on offer, they don't even consider whether meat is on the menu. Many of them probably feel healthier without meat but will indulge in it occasionally, and they don't mind if their soup has been made with chicken stock or their dessert with gelatine.

This book has been written in response to the change in our eating habits and caters for both vegetarians and virtual vegetarians. It attempts to switch the emphasis from meat to vegetables: so instead of recipes for meat or fish with occasional vegetarian options, it contains vegetarian recipes with suggestions on how to include meat or fish if that is what you feel like eating. If you are a vegetarian you will find most of the recipes are suitable for you. A few use chicken stock or gelatine because I find they give a better result in some cases but you can, of course, substitute vegetarian equivalents where appropriate.

I hope this book will finally put an end to the notion that vegetarian food cannot have the same depth of flavour as meat cookery. I am a meat eater myself, yet I believe that many of the secrets of good flavour lie with vegetables – from the root vegetables such as onions, garlic, carrots and celery that form the basis of many classic meat dishes, to pungent ingredients such as wild mushrooms and fresh herbs and spices. Techniques such as roasting or chargrilling intensify vegetable flavours and bring out their natural sweetness, while the current fashion for mixing and matching flavourings from different continents has, when done with care and discretion, greatly enhanced vegetarian cooking. And of course, let's not forget that many classic luxury ingredients are vegetarian – think of truffles, artichokes and asparagus, for example.

The recipes in this book vary in complexity but none should be beyond the ability of a reasonably experienced – or even just reasonably enthusiastic – cook. There is a big difference between cooking in a restaurant with a back-up team and producing food for family and friends at home, so although most of these recipes have appeared on my restaurant menus I have adapted them to make them suitable for the amateur cook. Some (but by no means all) feature expensive or unusual ingredients or have quite a lengthy preparation time, but this can make all the difference to a special meal – there are no short cuts to good food and I hope you'll find it's worth making the effort.

If you are daunted by the idea of producing a vegetarian main course you will find this book very flexible: either choose one main course and follow a traditional meal structure or combine two or three complementary dishes – perhaps a salad and a light dish from Chapter 3 with a vegetable accompaniment. A selection of first courses can also be served together to form a main course. This relaxed way of eating works particularly well with dishes that have a Mediterranean or Middle Eastern influence.

Virtually Vegetarian represents the fruits (and vegetables) of my labours in an exciting and challenging area of cookery, for which I have developed a real enthusiasm. I hope it will inspire vegetarians and meat eaters alike.

Note on the Recipes
- All recipes serve 4 unless otherwise stated
- Herbs are fresh unless otherwise stated
- Eggs are free-range size 3
- Both metric and Imperial measures are given; use either but do not combine the two
- **N.V. Suggestions** are non-vegetarian suggestions
- **Wine Notes** have been included in the recipes where appropriate

Paul Gayler

Cocktail Appetizers, First Courses and Soups

In a satisfying meal, the first course is very important since it should not only whet the appetite but also excite the tastebuds and set the style of the food to come.

First courses should generally be light in composition as they are usually followed by something more substantial.

One of the great advantages of cold first courses over hot is that they may be largely prepared ahead of time, thus relieving a lot of pressure when guests arrive, and allowing you more time to play the perfect host.

In this section I have also included some suggestions for cocktail appetizers to serve with aperitifs, which make an unexpected treat for your guests.

*A*ubergine and Dill Pirozhkis

If you make these little pastries larger they can be served as a hearty main course. They are best hot but can also be eaten cold.

*1 quantity of Basic Shortcrust Pastry
(see page 155) or 400g/14oz puff pastry
3 tbsp extra virgin olive oil
1 onion, finely chopped
1 clove garlic, crushed
¼ tsp fennel seeds
2 aubergines, finely diced
1 tbsp chopped dill
about 4 tbsp fresh white breadcrumbs
2 tbsp soured cream or crème fraîche
1 egg beaten with 1 tbsp milk or
water, to glaze*

MAKES ABOUT 20

Roll out the pastry thinly on a lightly floured surface then, using a small plain cutter, cut out 5–8 cm/2–3 inch rounds. Place them in the refrigerator while you prepare the filling. Preheat the oven to 200°C (400°F, Gas Mark 6).

Heat the oil in a pan, add the onion, garlic and fennel seeds and cook until lightly browned. Stir in the aubergine and sauté until soft and tender. Add the dill and then stir in enough breadcrumbs to bind the mixture together. Stir in the soured cream or crème fraîche and leave to cool.

Place a little of the cooled filling in the centre of each pastry round, brush the edges with the beaten egg, then pull the pastry up over the filling and pinch the edges together to form little pasties. Place on a baking sheet, brush with a little more beaten egg, and bake in the preheated oven for 12–15 minutes, until golden brown.

> ### N.V.
> ### *Suggestion*
>
> **Add 40g/1½oz chopped anchovies to the filling.**

*C*ocktail Tomatoes with Broad Bean Guacamole

If you haven't got time to stuff tomatoes, the broad bean guacamole makes an excellent dip.

*20 red cherry tomatoes or yellow pear tomatoes, or a mixture
50g/2oz cooked broad beans
(fresh or frozen)
2 tbsp yogurt
1 small green chilli, finely chopped
1 tbsp chopped coriander leaves
1 tbsp chopped onion*

*1 tsp fresh lime juice
a pinch of ground cumin
a pinch of ground coriander
salt and freshly ground black pepper
coriander leaves, to garnish*

Slice the top 8mm/⅜ inch off each tomato and carefully scoop out and discard the seeds. Reserve the tops.

To make the guacamole, place the broad beans in a bowl and mash them thoroughly with a fork. Stir in all the remaining ingredients except the whole coriander leaves and then season to taste with salt and pepper.

Fill each tomato with the guacamole, replace the tops and serve, garnished with coriander leaves.

Black Bean Caviar

This can be served simply with toasted baguette croutons, as a dip, or as a tasty appetizer, accompanied by Courgette Fritters (see page 114) and crème fraîche.

300g/11oz black turtle beans, soaked overnight and then drained
200g/7oz ripe tomatoes, peeled, deseeded and finely chopped
2 small cloves garlic, crushed
2 tbsp extra virgin olive oil
50g/2oz onion, finely chopped
½ small red chilli, finely chopped
1 tbsp chopped coriander leaves
1 tbsp champagne vinegar
2 tbsp fresh lime juice
salt and freshly ground black pepper
1 heaped tsp ground cumin, or to taste

Put the black turtle beans in a pan, cover them with fresh water and bring to the boil. Reduce the heat and simmer for about an hour, until tender, then drain and cool.

Coarsely chop the beans in a food processor, then transfer them to a bowl and stir in all the remaining ingredients. Chill in the refrigerator for about 1½–2 hours before serving.

Goat's Cheese and Olive Gougères

These gougères make a very good light appetizer and I have also served them as an accompaniment to minestrone. They can be filled with contrasting cheese fillings, such as ricotta or cream cheese with chives. Leave them to cool, then make a small hole in the bottom of each one and use a piping bag fitted with a thin nozzle to insert your chosen filling.

200ml/7fl oz water
75g/3oz unsalted butter
100g/4oz plain flour
2 eggs, beaten
75g/3oz soft goat's cheese
25g/1oz black olives, finely chopped
salt and freshly ground black pepper
a little freshly grated Parmesan cheese (optional)

Preheat the oven to 180°C (350°F, Gas Mark 4). Bring the water and butter to the boil in a pan and then gently rain in the flour, beating the mixture with a wooden spoon until it is smooth and leaves the sides of the pan clean. Leave to cool, then add the eggs a little at a time, beating well between each addition. Mash the goat's cheese with a fork, stir it in to the dough with the olives and then season to taste.

Using a piping bag fitted with a 1cm/½ inch plain nozzle, pipe the mixture in little 2.5cm/1 inch lozenges on a buttered baking sheet, leaving 2.5–5cm/1–2 inches between each one. Dust them with the Parmesan, if using, and bake in the preheated oven for 15–20 minutes until golden brown, well risen and crisp on the outside. Cool slightly before serving.

> ### N.V.
> *Suggestion*
>
> **Add 25g/1oz chopped anchovy fillets to the basic mixture.**

WINE NOTES

A young Pinotage from South Africa

Cocktail Tomatoes with Broad Bean Guacamole (page 12), Mini Cornmeal Pizzas, Baby Jacket Potatoes with Mushrooms and Gribiche Sauce, and Tofu, Onion and Cumin Samosas (both on page 16)

Mini Cornmeal Pizzas

The dough for these pizzas is very quick to make and doesn't need a long rising time.

7g/¼oz fresh yeast
125ml/4fl oz warm milk
150g/5oz plain flour
75g/3oz fine cornmeal
2 tsp extra virgin olive oil, plus extra for brushing
½ tsp sugar
½ tsp salt

MAKES ABOUT 20

Place the yeast, warm milk and 50g/2oz of the flour in a bowl and mix to a smooth batter. Cover lightly with the remaining flour and sprinkle the cornmeal over it.

Leave in a warm place for about 10 minutes until the ferment has broken through the flour and cornmeal, then stir in the oil, sugar and salt. Mix all the ingredients together on a lightly floured surface to form a dough, but do not knead it. Leave the dough to rest under a damp cloth for a few minutes. Preheat the oven to 180°C (350°F, Gas Mark 4).

Roll out the dough until it is 5mm/¼ inch thick and cut it into 6cm/2½ inch rounds with a pastry cutter. Brush each round with a little oil, then place on a baking sheet and leave in a warm place for 10 minutes or until slightly risen.

Add any of the suggested toppings (opposite) and bake in the preheated oven until golden. Serve immediately.

SPINACH, MUSHROOM AND GORGONZOLA

Sautéed spinach and mushrooms, topped with diced sun-dried tomatoes and Gorgonzola cheese.

ROASTED PEPPERS, RED ONION AND GOAT'S CHEESE

Diced roasted red peppers with crumbled goat's cheese, red onion rings and fresh or dried oregano.

ARTICHOKE WITH TOMATO TAPENADE, AUBERGINE AND ROASTED GARLIC

A base of Tomato or Black Olive Tapenade (see page 153), topped with sautéed artichokes and aubergine, slivers of roasted garlic and chopped basil.

DRIED FRUIT WITH SPINACH AND MOZZARELLA

Sautéed spinach, diced soaked dried apricots and prunes, and cubed mozzarella cheese.

WINE NOTES

A young Nebbiolo or Chianti

Baby Jacket Potatoes with Mushrooms and Gribiche sauce

You can use cultivated or wild mushrooms for this, depending on what is available.

20 baby new potatoes, preferably
Jersey Royals
salt and freshly ground black pepper
3 tbsp extra virgin olive oil
1 clove garlic, crushed
1 shallot, finely chopped
100g/4oz mushrooms, cut into
5mm/¼ inch dice

125ml/4fl oz Gribiche Sauce (see
page 153)
sprigs of parsley, to garnish

Preheat the oven to 200°C (400°F, Gas Mark 6). Prick the potatoes with a cocktail stick, salt them lightly and place them on a baking sheet. Bake them for 20–25 minutes or until tender, then leave to cool.

With a sharp knife cut a small slice off the base of each potato to allow them to sit flat. Then cut a thin slice off the top of each potato; scoop out and discard the flesh to form a cavity for the mushroom filling.

Heat the oil in a pan, add the garlic and shallot and cook for 1 minute. Add the mushrooms and sauté for 2 minutes, then season to taste.

Spoon the mushroom filling into the potatoes. Place a small spoonful of gribiche sauce on top, garnish with parsley and serve immediately.

Tofu, Onion and Cumin Samosas

The onion and cumin filling also makes an excellent appetizer spread on thin flutes of toasted French bread, topped with goat's cheese and browned under a hot grill.

50g/2oz unsalted butter
2 onions, finely sliced
½ tbsp cumin seeds, plus extra for
sprinkling
salt and freshly ground black pepper
8 sheets of filo pastry, about 30 × 24cm/
12 × 8 inches
4 tbsp clarified butter (see page 151)
75g/3oz tofu, cut into 8mm/⅜ inch dice

MAKES 16

Preheat the oven to 180°C (350°F, Gas Mark 4). Heat the butter in a small saucepan, add the onions and cook gently until golden brown and tender. Add the cumin seeds and cook for a further 2 minutes, then season to taste and leave to cool.

Cut the sheets of filo pastry width-ways into strips about 6cm/2½ inches wide, then stack up the strips and cover them with a damp cloth to prevent them drying out. Place 1 strip of filo pastry on a damp work surface, brush with clarified butter, then place another strip on top and brush with more butter. Place 1 teaspoon of the onion mixture at one end of the filo, top with a little diced tofu, then fold one corner diagonally over it to make a triangle; keep folding until you reach the end of the strip. Repeat with the remaining filo pastry and filling.

Brush a baking sheet with a little clarified butter and place the samosas on it; sprinkle with a few cumin seeds and bake in the preheated oven for 8–10 minutes, until golden.

N. V.
Suggestion

Replace the tofu with chopped anchovies, or with diced chicken livers, cleaned and sautéed in a little hot oil for 2 minutes and then drained and seasoned.

Sichuan Barbecued Aubergine Rolls with Papaya and Cucumber

3 tbsp good-quality red wine vinegar,
such as Cabernet Sauvignon
1 tbsp honey
1 tbsp ketjap manis (sweet Indonesian
soy sauce)
2 tbsp vegetable oil
4 tsp sesame oil
salt and freshly ground black pepper
2 medium aubergines, cut lengthways
into slices 8mm/⅜ inch thick
1 small green chilli, deseeded and very
finely diced
½ tsp sesame seeds, toasted
1 tsp finely chopped fresh ginger root
1 tbsp chopped mint
2 tbsp chopped coriander leaves
1 papaya, peeled, deseeded and cut into
8mm/⅜ inch dice

½ cucumber, peeled and cut into
8mm/⅜ inch dice
coriander leaves, to garnish

Mix together the vinegar, honey, ketjap manis and the oils with a little seasoning and pour into a shallow dish. Marinate the aubergine slices in this mixture overnight.

The next day, remove the aubergine slices from the marinade and cook them on a barbecue for 2–3 minutes per side (or under a hot grill for 5 minutes per side), until tender and golden. Return the slices to the marinade and leave to cool.

Mix together the chilli, sesame seeds, ginger, herbs, papaya and cucumber and stir in a little of the marinade to bind. Season to taste.

Remove the aubergine slices from the marinade, place a little of the papaya and cucumber mixture near the top of each one, then roll them up and place them in a dish. Coat with a little of the remaining marinade, garnish with coriander and serve.

N.V. Suggestion

Add some prawns or even diced cooked lobster to the filling for a special treat.

Oriental Ratatouille

I love Asian flavours and I sometimes prepare a different ratatouille on this theme, with cumin seeds, fenugreek seeds and chopped coriander.

1 tbsp sesame oil
4 tbsp extra virgin olive oil
1 clove garlic, crushed
15g/½oz fresh ginger root, finely chopped
½ red pepper, diced
½ yellow pepper, diced
1 large courgette, diced
50g/2oz daikon radish (mooli), diced

1 small aubergine, diced
600g/1lb 6oz plum tomatoes, peeled,
deseeded and diced
½ tsp sugar
salt and freshly ground black pepper
10 green or opal basil leaves, shredded
soy sauce (optional)

Heat the sesame oil and olive oil in a pan, add the garlic and ginger and cook gently until they give off their aroma. Add all the vegetables except the tomatoes and sauté over a high heat for 2–3 minutes. Then add the tomatoes and sugar and cook for another half minute. The vegetables should not be browned and should retain their crispness.

Season to taste and add the shredded basil, then transfer the mixture to a bowl and leave to cool. If you like, season with a dash of soy sauce for a little more piquancy.

Peking Soused Vegetables

This is an adaptation of vegetables à la grecque, with oriental flavours.

100g/4oz cauliflower, cut into small florets
12 baby carrots, lightly scraped
8 baby sweetcorn
6 small spring onions, trimmed (leave on some of the green)
25g/1oz beansprouts
75g/3oz cucumber, peeled, deseeded and cut into 2.5 × 1cm/1 × ½ inch batons
75g/3oz shiitake mushrooms
salt and freshly ground black pepper

FOR THE MARINADE
1 litre/1¾ pints water
2 cloves garlic, thinly sliced
1 small bay leaf
1 sprig of thyme
6 coriander seeds
40g/1½oz fresh ginger root, thinly sliced
2 star anise
15g/½oz sugar
4 tbsp rice wine vinegar
2 lemon grass stalks, roughly chopped
juice of 1 lemon
20 large coriander leaves
4 tbsp vegetable oil

Place all the marinade ingredients except the oil in a saucepan and bring to the boil. Add a little salt and simmer for 10 minutes, then stir in the oil. Add the cauliflower florets and simmer for 3 minutes; add the carrots, sweetcorn and spring onions and cook for a further 2 minutes. Finally, add the beansprouts, cucumber and mushrooms and cook until only just tender. It is important that all the vegetables retain a little crunchiness. Remove the vegetables from the pan with a slotted spoon and set aside to cool. Strain the cooking liquid and chill. Pick out any marinade ingredients from the vegetables, reserving the coriander leaves and seeds. Adjust the seasoning.

To serve, transfer the vegetables to a serving dish, moisten with a little of the chilled marinade and garnish with the reserved coriander seeds and leaves.

N.V.
Suggestion

Add medallions of lobster to the marinated vegetables for a real treat.

Stir-fried Asparagus with Ginger and Black Sesame Seeds

This is one of the best ways of cooking asparagus because it retains its crispness.

3 tbsp vegetable oil
1 tbsp sesame oil
25g/1oz fresh ginger root, thinly sliced
900g/2lb young green asparagus spears, trimmed and cut into 6cm/2½ inch lengths
1 tbsp light soy sauce
a pinch of brown sugar
salt and freshly ground black pepper
2 tbsp rice wine vinegar
1 tsp black sesame seeds

Heat the oils in a wok or frying pan, add the ginger and cook for 1 minute. Add the asparagus and stir-fry for 2 minutes, until it is just tender but still slightly crisp. Stir in the soy sauce and sugar, season to taste and then leave to cool. Add the rice wine vinegar and mix together. Sprinkle with sesame seeds and serve.

*A*sian Antipasti: Sichuan Barbecued Aubergine Rolls with Papaya and Cucumber (page 17), Stir-fried Asparagus with
Ginger and Black Sesame Seeds, Peking Soused Vegetables, Grilled Vegetable Satay (page 21), Iceberg Lettuce Rolls (page 20)

Iceberg Lettuce Rolls

The shredded vegetables in this recipe can be prepared very quickly if you use a mandoline. Pink pickled ginger adds a distinctive flavour but can be omitted if it is unobtainable.

1 carrot, shredded into fine strips
1 courgette, shredded into fine strips
1 red pepper, shredded into fine strips
4 spring onions, shredded into fine strips
50g/2oz beansprouts
25g/1oz fresh ginger root, finely chopped
2 cloves garlic, crushed
4 tbsp vegetable oil
1 tbsp sesame oil
juice of ½ lime
salt and freshly ground black pepper
1 iceberg lettuce, leaves separated
15g/½oz pink pickled ginger
Asian Dipping Sauce (see page 154)

FOR THE ORIENTAL REMOULADE SAUCE
4 tbsp thick mayonnaise (see page 52)
1 tsp light soy sauce
¼ tsp deseeded and finely chopped red chilli
1 tbsp chopped coriander leaves

To make the filling, combine all the ingredients except the lettuce, pickled ginger and Asian dipping sauce in a bowl, season lightly and leave for 1 hour to soften. In a separate bowl, mix together all the ingredients for the sauce and season to taste.

Drain the vegetables well, then set half of them aside for the garnish. Stir enough of the oriental remoulade sauce into the remaining vegetables to bind them, then adjust the seasoning, adding salt and pepper to taste.

Fill each lettuce leaf with the mixture, then top with 2 wafer-thin pieces of pickled ginger and roll up like a cigar, trimming any untidy edges. Arrange the rolls on a serving plate, seam-side down, scatter the reserved vegetables over the top and serve accompanied by Asian dipping sauce.

I think the best way to serve these is to let each guest roll up their own rolls, which should be dipped into the sauce and eaten with the fingers.

N.V.
Suggestion

Add fresh white crabmeat to the vegetable mixture.

Artichokes with Parmesan Bread Sauce

8 medium globe artichokes
100ml/3½ fl oz extra virgin olive oil
175ml/6fl oz dry white wine
300ml/½ pint water
juice of 2 lemons
3 cloves garlic, 2 crushed and 1 halved
a little coarsely cracked black pepper

FOR THE SAUCE
50g/2oz stale white bread, made into very fine breadcrumbs

50g/2oz Parmesan cheese, very finely grated
150ml/¼ pint extra virgin olive oil
1 heaped tablespoon chopped parsley

Prepare the artichokes as described on page 138 but peel the stems and trim them to 4cm/1½ inches in length.

Combine the oil, wine, water, lemon juice and crushed garlic in a saucepan and bring to the boil. Reduce the heat, add the artichokes and simmer for 12–14 minutes, until tender. Remove the artichokes with a slotted spoon and leave to cool. Cut them lengthways into halves or quarters.

Mix together all the ingredients for the sauce. Just before serving, rub 4 serving plates with the halved garlic clove, then lightly coat each plate with a little of the sauce. Arrange the artichokes on top, season with a little coarsely cracked pepper and serve at room temperature.

Grilled Vegetable Satay

100g/4oz pumpkin, peeled and cut into
large dice
100g/4oz turnips, peeled and cut into
large dice
75g/3oz button mushrooms
150g/5oz cauliflower, cut into
small florets
½ aubergine, cut into large dice

FOR THE MARINADE
3 tbsp ketjap manis (sweet Indonesian
soy sauce)
1 tbsp grated fresh ginger root
juice of 2 lemons
1 lemon grass stalk, crushed (optional)
2 cloves garlic, crushed
3 tbsp vegetable oil
salt and freshly ground black pepper

FOR THE PEANUT SAUCE
2 tbsp groundnut or vegetable oil
2 cloves garlic, crushed
1 small red chilli, deseeded and chopped
2 tbsp brown sugar
2 tbsp light soy sauce
175g/6oz crunchy peanut butter
1 tbsp lemon juice
100ml/3½fl oz coconut milk

Put 12–16 thin bamboo skewers in water to soak; this prevents them charring during cooking. Mix all the marinade ingredients together in a bowl and set aside.

Thread the vegetables on to the skewers and place them in a shallow dish; season, then pour the marinade over them. Leave to marinate at room temperature for up to 4 hours.

To make the peanut sauce, heat the oil in a small pan and add the garlic and chilli. Cook for 1–2 minutes, then add the brown sugar and soy sauce and stir until the sugar has dissolved. Mix in the peanut butter and lemon juice, then pour in the coconut milk. Bring to the boil, stir and simmer for about 10 minutes or until the mixture thickens. Season to taste.

Remove the vegetable skewers from the marinade, brushing off any clinging marinade ingredients. Place the skewers on a barbecue or under a very hot grill and cook, turning frequently, until all the vegetables are charred on the outside but soft and succulent inside. Serve them immediately with the peanut sauce as a dip, which can be warm or cold.

N.V. Suggestion

A variety of meat or shellfish may be added to the skewers: try cubes of chicken, pork or lamb, or prawns, langoustines or pieces of lobster or monkfish.

WINE NOTES

A white Viognier from the Côteaux de l'Ardeche or, for a special occasion, a Condrieu

Caponata Charlottes with Dried Fruits

This recipe looks long and complex but in fact it is quite simple to prepare and most stages can be made well in advance. Mozzarella can be substituted for the goat's cheese. There will be some caponata left over after filling the moulds; it makes a good light meal with some crusty bread.

2 large aubergines, cut lengthways into
slices 5mm/¼ inch thick
olive oil for brushing
salt and freshly ground black pepper
2 crottin de Chavignol goat's cheeses, or
other small, firm goat's cheeses, cut in
half horizontally

FOR THE CAPONATA
2 tbsp extra virgin olive oil
1 red onion, cut into 1cm/½ inch dice
1 clove garlic, crushed
1 small aubergine, cut into 1cm/
½ inch dice
½ red pepper, cut into 1cm/½ inch dice
½ yellow pepper, cut into 1cm/
½ inch dice
2 small courgettes, cut into 1cm/
½ inch dice
1 celery stick, cut into 1cm/½ inch dice
25g/1oz dried apricots, soaked for up to
2 hours and then cut into 1cm/
½ inch dice
25g/1oz dried apples, soaked for up to
2 hours and then cut into 1cm/
½ inch dice
2 tbsp balsamic vinegar
2 tbsp maple syrup or honey

1 tbsp raisins, soaked in warm water
until plump
3 tbsp pine kernels
salt and freshly ground black pepper

FOR THE TOMATO OIL
4 ripe plum tomatoes
1 small clove garlic, halved
1 sprig of thyme
4 tbsp extra virgin olive oil
a pinch of sugar (optional)

FOR THE GARNISH
20–30 small rocket leaves
2 tomatoes, peeled, deseeded and cut into
1cm/½ inch diamonds

Preheat the oven to 180°C (350°F, Gas Mark 4). Place the aubergine slices on a baking sheet and brush them with olive oil. Season, and bake for about 8 minutes or until tender. Remove the aubergine slices from the oven and leave to cool, but leave the oven on.

Use the aubergine slices to line 4 ramekin dishes, each about 175ml/6fl oz in capacity; it is important that the slices overlap each other, leaving no gaps, and that they hang over the rim of the dish so that they can be used to cover and secure the caponata filling.

To make the caponata, heat the olive oil in a pan and add the onion and garlic. Cook for 1 minute before adding the remaining vegetables and

the dried fruit. Cook over a moderate heat for about 10 minutes or until the vegetables are softened and lightly golden. Add the balsamic vinegar, maple syrup or honey, and the raisins and mix in well to form a sort of sweet and sour sauce. Finally, add the pine kernels and season to taste.

Put a 1cm/½ inch layer of caponata into the aubergine-lined dishes. Top with a piece of goat's cheese, followed by more caponata. Fold over the aubergine slices to secure the filling and press them down to ensure the filling is compact. Place on a baking sheet and bake for 4–5 minutes, until just warmed through.

To make the tomato oil, cut the tomatoes in quarters and extract all the juice using a juice extractor or a blender (see page 146). Strain the tomato juice into a small pan and add the garlic and thyme. Bring to the boil, then reduce the heat to a simmer and cook until the liquid is reduced to half its original volume.

Remove from the heat, strain the juice again and leave to cool. Whisk in the olive oil, season and add a pinch of sugar if necessary. (This oil may be made 3–4 days in advance and kept in the refrigerator.)

To serve, carefully unmould the warm charlottes on to serving plates, garnish with the rocket and diced tomatoes and pour around a little of the tomato oil.

*S*tuffed Mushrooms with Curried Lentils and Indian Tomato Salsa *(page 25), Caponata Charlottes with Dried Fruits, and Baked Figs with Spinach, Almonds and Gorgonzola (page 24)*

*B*aked Figs with Spinach, Almonds and Gorgonzola

8 fresh figs
50g/2oz unsalted butter
25g/1oz onion, finely chopped
3 tbsp flaked almonds
1 small clove garlic, crushed
a pinch of fennel seeds
50g/2oz chestnut mushrooms,
roughly chopped
150g/5oz fresh spinach
50g/2oz Gorgonzola cheese, finely diced
50g/2oz Parmesan cheese, finely grated
salt and freshly ground black pepper

FOR THE SAUCE
5 tbsp vegetable stock (see page 148)
150ml/¼ pint double cream
125g/4½oz Gorgonzola cheese,
finely diced
50g/2oz chilled unsalted butter, cut
into small pieces
½ bunch of watercress, stalks removed
and leaves finely chopped

*P*reheat the oven to 180°C (350°F, Gas Mark 4). Cut the figs in half vertically and, using a teaspoon or a melon baller, carefully scoop out a little flesh from the centre of each fig, without destroying its shape. Chop the removed flesh and set aside.

Melt half the butter in a frying pan, add the onion, almonds and garlic and cook over a gentle heat until golden. Remove from the heat and leave the mixture to cool.

Heat the remaining butter in a saucepan, add the fennel seeds and mushrooms and cook over a high heat to seal in the juices. Add the spinach and lower the heat to allow the spinach to wilt. Drain well and leave to cool, then chop finely and place in a bowl. Add the onion, almond and garlic mixture, the Gorgonzola, half the Parmesan, and the reserved fig flesh. Season to taste.

Fill the fig halves with this mixture and place them in a lightly buttered baking dish. Sprinkle the tops with the remaining Parmesan cheese and bake in the preheated oven for 10–12 minutes, until just soft.

Meanwhile, make the sauce: place the vegetable stock and cream in a pan and boil until reduced to half its original volume. Whisk in the Gorgonzola cheese until melted, then finally whisk in the butter to form a smooth sauce. Stir in the watercress and season to taste. Pour the sauce into a dish, arrange the figs on top and serve.

N.V.
Suggestion

Add some diced prosciutto to the filling for the figs.

WINE NOTES

A young Cabernet Sauvignon from South Africa

Stuffed Mushrooms with Curried Lentils and Indian Tomato Salsa

This recipe calls for large chestnut mushrooms but button mushrooms are fine if you can find ones that are big enough. The important thing is that they should be cup-shaped to hold the filling.

150g/5oz green lentils, soaked overnight
and then drained
8 very large chestnut mushrooms
3 tbsp extra virgin olive oil
½ onion, finely chopped
1 clove garlic, crushed
1 level tbsp Home-made Curry Powder
(see page 154)
75g/3oz spinach, cooked and
finely chopped
1 tbsp chopped coriander leaves
1 tbsp red wine vinegar
3 tbsp fresh white breadcrumbs
1 tbsp yogurt
coriander leaves, to garnish

FOR THE SALSA
6 green tomatoes, deseeded and cut into
8mm/⅜ inch dice
2 spring onions, shredded
1 tbsp chopped coriander leaves
1 green chilli, deseeded and
finely chopped
juice of 1 lime
1 tsp caster sugar
salt and freshly ground black pepper

Place the lentils in a saucepan, cover with water and bring to the boil, then reduce the heat and simmer until tender. Make the salsa: mix all the ingredients together and leave to stand for at least 30 minutes (it may be made a day in advance if necessary).

Remove about two-thirds of the lentils from the pan, drain them and set aside. Continue cooking the remainder until they are very soft and mushy, then drain them and blitz in a liquidizer to form a smooth, thick purée. Preheat the oven to 200°C (400°F, Gas Mark 6).

Remove the stalks from the mushrooms and set the mushroom caps aside. Chop the stalks finely. Heat the oil in a frying pan, add the onion, garlic and chopped mushroom stalks and cook for about 3 minutes, until golden. Add the curry powder, reduce the heat and cook for a further 5 minutes. Add the whole cooked lentils, spinach, coriander and vinegar and mix together. Then stir in the breadcrumbs and enough of the lentil purée to bind the mixture together. Add the yogurt and season to taste.

Fill the mushroom caps with the curried lentil mixture and place them on a baking sheet. Bake them in the preheated oven for 15–20 minutes, until the mushrooms are tender. Arrange the mushrooms on serving plates, garnish with coriander and serve immediately, accompanied by the salsa.

WINE NOTES

A spicy Alsace white or Pinot Gris

Mushroom Tartare with Marinated Baby Leeks in Champagne Vinegar

3 tbsp sherry vinegar or red wine
vinegar
2 shallots, finely chopped
1 small clove garlic, crushed
juice of ½ orange
50g/2oz chestnut mushrooms
75g/3oz small oyster mushrooms
50g/2oz button mushrooms
salt and freshly ground black pepper
2 tbsp finely chopped mixed herbs, such as
parsley, basil, thyme and rosemary
½ tsp Dijon mustard
½ tsp tomato ketchup
3 tbsp walnut oil

FOR THE LEEKS
20 baby leeks, trimmed
5 tbsp champagne vinegar
150ml/¼ pint extra virgin olive oil
a pinch of sugar

Put the vinegar, shallots, garlic and orange juice in a pan, bring to the boil and then remove from the heat. Grill all the mushrooms until tender, season lightly and add to this marinade. Leave to cool.

Remove the mushrooms from the marinade and chop them fairly finely, reserving some whole oyster mushrooms for garnish. Place the chopped mushrooms in a bowl, add the herbs, mustard and tomato ketchup and season to taste. Stir in a spoonful of the mushroom marinade together with all the walnut oil.

Cook the baby leeks in boiling salted water for 1 minute, then drain them thoroughly and place in a shallow dish. Mix together the champagne vinegar, oil and sugar and pour over the leeks. Leave to cool.

To serve, place a small round pastry cutter or ring in the centre of each serving plate, pack them tightly with the mushroom tartare and then remove the rings and garnish with the marinated leeks and reserved oyster mushrooms.

N.V.
Suggestion

Add some shredded duck confit to the mushroom tartare, or serve topped with a piece of soused mackerel or sea bass at room temperature.

WINE NOTES

A red Loire such as Chinon

Shiitake Mushroom Salad with Thai Vinaigrette

Another marinated mushroom dish, this time with oriental flavours. The long list of ingredients may look daunting at first but don't despair; it's very quick to put together.

FOR THE MARINATED MUSHROOMS
200g/7oz shiitake mushrooms
1 small clove garlic, crushed
4 tbsp extra virgin olive oil
1 tbsp sesame oil
¼ tsp sugar
2 tbsp light soy sauce
2 tbsp balsamic vinegar
salt and freshly ground black pepper

FOR THE VINAIGRETTE
2 tbsp balsamic vinegar
5 tbsp rice wine vinegar
2 tbsp extra virgin olive oil
2 tbsp maple syrup
¼ tsp crushed garlic
12 coriander seeds, coarsely crushed
6 mint leaves, roughly chopped
1 small red chilli, finely chopped
2 tsp black sesame seeds

FOR THE SALAD
100g/4oz Chinese cabbage, finely shredded
2 carrots, finely shredded
25g/1oz mangetout, finely shredded
75g/3oz beansprouts
2 large spring onions, finely shredded
1 tbsp finely shredded fresh ginger root
25g/1oz dry-roasted peanuts
12 coriander leaves

Brush the shiitake mushrooms free of any dirt but don't wash them as they absorb water like a sponge. Cut them into small wedges.

Put the garlic, oils, sugar, soy sauce, vinegar and seasoning in a small pan and bring to the boil. Remove from the heat, pour over the mushrooms and leave to marinate for up to an hour. Meanwhile, mix together all the ingredients for the vinaigrette, adding seasoning to taste.

Place all the ingredients for the salad in a bowl, add sufficient vinaigrette to dress the vegetables lightly and adjust the seasoning if necessary. Divide the salad between 4 serving plates, surround with the marinated mushrooms and drizzle with a little of the remaining vinaigrette. Chill thoroughly before serving.

N.V. Suggestion

Add some shredded cooked chicken breast or flaked fresh crabmeat to the vegetables.

WINE NOTES

A spicy, rich Australian white, such as a late-harvest Riesling

Devilled Chestnut Mushrooms with Garlic and Mint

Chestnut mushrooms are sometimes known as Portabello or straw mushrooms. Their dark flesh is strong and meaty, rather like flat mushrooms.

6 tbsp extra virgin olive oil
1 tbsp balsamic vinegar
2 tbsp lemon juice
a few drops of Worcestershire sauce
10 large mint leaves, chopped
salt

450g/1lb chestnut mushrooms (or large button mushrooms)
2 cloves garlic, very thinly sliced
1 tbsp black peppercorns, coarsely crushed

Make a marinade by mixing 4 tablespoons of the oil with the vinegar, lemon juice, Worcestershire sauce and mint. Add salt to taste.

Wipe the mushrooms with a damp cloth (do not wash them) and cut small slits in them with a sharp knife approximately 1cm/½ inch apart, then insert the garlic slivers. Brush the mushrooms with the remaining oil and then sprinkle them with the crushed black peppercorns and a little salt.

Heat a frying pan until very hot, add the mushrooms and sauté them for about 2 minutes, until golden. Transfer them to a bowl, pour on the marinade and leave in the fridge for 24 hours. You can serve them whole or slice them before serving.

Mousseline of Haricot Beans

Sometimes I garnish this mousseline with marinated artichoke hearts and fresh truffles – a marriage of rich and poor! If you do this, omit the olives from the dressing. It's also good served simply with some baguette croutons.

250g/9oz dried haricot beans, soaked overnight and then drained
1 bouquet garni
4 tbsp extra virgin olive oil
4 cloves garlic, crushed
2 gelatine leaves (or vegetarian equivalent)
250ml/8fl oz milk
4 tbsp double cream, semi-whipped
1 tbsp lemon juice
salt and freshly ground black pepper

FOR THE DRESSING
2 tbsp extra virgin olive oil
1 tbsp sherry vinegar
1 tsp finely chopped black olives

Cook the beans in boiling water with the bouquet garni for about 1¼ hours or until they are very soft and mushy. Drain them, reserving 2 tablespoons of the cooking liquid for the dressing.

Heat 1 tablespoon of the oil in a pan, add the garlic and beans and cook for 2 minutes.

Put the gelatine in a small bowl, cover with water and leave to soak for 5 minutes. Warm the milk and dissolve the gelatine in it, then pour it on to the beans in the pan. Bring to the boil, then transfer to a blender and liquidize to a very smooth purée (for an even smoother mousse pass the purée through a fine sieve).

When the purée is just warm, fold in the semi-whipped cream, the remaining oil, lemon juice and seasoning to taste. Transfer the mixture to a bowl and leave to set in the refrigerator until required.

Blend the ingredients for the dressing together with the reserved bean liquid and season to taste.

To serve, remove the mousseline of haricot beans from the fridge and, using an ice-cream scoop or a spoon, place one scoop in the centre of each serving plate and drizzle a little of the dressing around.

Escabeche of Courgettes with Olives and Saffron

virgin olive oil for frying
450g/1lb medium courgettes, cut
lengthways into slices 1cm/½ inch thick
2 cloves garlic, thinly sliced
salt and freshly ground black pepper

FOR THE DRESSING
1 tbsp honey
1 tbsp lightly crushed coriander seeds
a good pinch of saffron
2 tbsp sherry vinegar
8 tbsp extra virgin olive oil
10 basil leaves, chopped
6 black olives, stoned and chopped

Pour a film of olive oil over the base of a large frying pan, heat gently and then add the courgette slices. Sauté them until they begin to soften and are very lightly coloured. Do not crowd the pan; cook the courgettes in batches if necessary. Transfer them to a shallow dish and strew over the garlic slices, then season.

Put the honey, coriander and saffron in a small saucepan with 4 tablespoons of water and bring to the boil, then leave over a low heat for 1–2 minutes for the saffron to infuse. Remove from the heat and cool slightly. Whisk in the vinegar and then the oil to form a warm vinaigrette dressing. Add the basil and olives and season to taste. Pour the dressing over the courgettes and leave to marinate for up to 4 hours at room temperature.

WINE NOTES

**A South African
Sauvignon Blanc**

Stuffed Plum Tomatoes with Mozzarella in Sicilian Sauce

This simple Sicilian sauce is known as salmoriglio and it is usually served as an accompaniment to fish, meat and vegetables.

8 ripe plum tomatoes
1 clove garlic, crushed
salt and freshly ground black pepper
100g/4oz buffalo mozzarella cheese, diced
75g/3oz fresh white breadcrumbs

FOR THE SAUCE
200ml/7fl oz extra virgin olive oil
½ tbsp chopped flat-leaf parsley
1 tbsp oregano
2 cloves garlic, crushed
juice of 2 lemons
6 tbsp hot water

Preheat the oven to 220°C (425°F, Gas Mark 7). Halve the tomatoes lengthways and scoop out the seeds and central membranes. Rub an ovenproof dish with the crushed garlic and lay the tomatoes in it cut side up. Season with salt and pepper.

Blend all the ingredients for the sauce together and season with salt and pepper. Drizzle about half the sauce over the tomatoes and bake them in the preheated oven for 5 minutes.

Remove from the oven, scatter the diced mozzarella and breadcrumbs over them and then bake for a further 5 minutes or until golden.

Pour the remaining sauce into a jug and serve it with the tomatoes.

WINE NOTES

An Italian red from Piedmont, such as Barbaresco

Salad Tart with Radicchio and Roasted Garlic

I sometimes serve this with a julienne of roasted red peppers in a champagne vinaigrette

1 quantity of Basic Shortcrust Pastry (see page 155) or Mashed Potato Pastry (see page 155)
8 large cloves garlic, unpeeled
40g/1½oz unsalted butter
1 head of radicchio, shredded
salt and freshly ground black pepper
2 eggs
2 egg yolks
50g/2oz ricotta cheese
300ml/½ pint double cream
200ml/7fl oz milk
freshly grated nutmeg

Preheat the oven to 180°C (350°F, Gas Mark 4). Roll out the pastry and use to line a 20cm/8 inch tart tin. Line with greaseproof paper, fill with cooking beans and bake blind for 8–10 minutes. Remove the paper and beans and return to the oven for a further 5 minutes, then leave to cool.

Wrap the garlic cloves in foil and bake them for 25–30 minutes until very tender. Peel off the skin and pass the garlic through a fine sieve.

Heat the butter in a pan, add the radicchio and cook gently for 2–3 minutes until softened. Season with salt and pepper and leave to cool.

Beat the eggs, egg yolks, ricotta and garlic purée together in a bowl and then add the cream and milk. Season with salt, pepper and nutmeg.

Arrange the raddichio in the pastry case and pour in the filling. Bake in the oven for 30–35 minutes or until set. Serve warm.

Poached Asparagus with Brown Butter Sabayon

32 green asparagus spears, trimmed and peeled
1 tbsp white wine vinegar
1 shallot, finely chopped
8 white peppercorns, coarsely crushed
3 egg yolks
150g/5oz clarified butter (see page 151)
juice of ½ lemon
salt and freshly ground black pepper
cayenne pepper
50g/2oz chilled butter, cut into small pieces

Divide the asparagus into 4 bunches, tie them together gently with string, then immerse them in a pot of boiling salted water. Cook for about 4–5 minutes, until just tender. Drain them well and keep warm.

To make the sabayon, place the wine vinegar, shallot and peppercorns in a pan over a low heat and cook until the vinegar is reduced to half its original volume. Allow to cool, then transfer to a bowl. Whisk in the egg yolks with 2 tablespoons of water and place the bowl over a pan of simmering water (the bottom of the bowl should not touch the water). Whisk continuously until the mixture thickens enough to leave a trail on the surface when dropped from the whisk. Using a ladle, gradually add the clarified butter in a thin stream, whisking constantly until all the butter is incorporated. Add the lemon juice and seasoning and strain through a fine sieve or, better still, a piece of butter muslin; keep the sabayon warm.

To finish, put the chilled butter in a frying pan and place over a high heat for about 30 seconds, until it foams, turns a nutty brown colour and gives off a nutty fragrance. Whisk the foaming butter into the sabayon sauce and blend well. Pour the sauce on to serving plates and serve the asparagus tips with it, for dipping.

Grilled Vegetable Ceviche with Fennel and Cumin Jam

Ceviche usually describes a method of pickling or marinating raw fish. Here vegetables are grilled and then marinated in a spicy dressing.

3 small peppers, 1 red, 1 yellow and 1 green
2 aubergines, cut into rounds 5mm/ ¼ inch thick
2 medium courgettes, cut into rounds 5mm/¼ inch thick
1 small red onion, cut into slices 8mm/ ⅜ inch thick
4 tbsp extra virgin olive oil
juice of 1 lemon
juice of 2 limes
½ tsp caster sugar
1 tsp crushed coriander seeds
2 tbsp chopped coriander leaves
½ tsp finely chopped red chilli
salt and freshly ground black pepper
coriander leaves, to garnish
12 baguette croutons (see page 34)

FOR THE FENNEL AND CUMIN JAM
3 tbsp extra virgin olive oil
1 fennel bulb, thinly sliced
½ onion, thinly sliced
2 cloves garlic, thinly sliced
1 tsp caster sugar
½ tsp ground cumin

Place the peppers under a hot grill or, better still, grill them on an open flame, until they begin to blister and turn black. Keep turning them to ensure that all sides are done. Remove from the heat and, when cool enough to handle, peel off the skin under cold running water. Cut the peppers in half and remove the seeds and inner membranes. Slice them thinly and place in a shallow dish.

Grill the aubergine, courgette and onion slices until golden brown and charred, then add them to the peppers.

In a bowl mix together the olive oil, lemon and lime juice, caster sugar, coriander seeds, chopped coriander, chilli and a little salt and pepper. Leave to stand for 5 minutes for the sugar to dissolve. Pour this marinade over the grilled vegetables and leave for 2–4 hours in a cool place.

To make the fennel and cumin jam, heat the olive oil in a heavy-based pan, add the fennel, onion and garlic, then cover and cook over a very low heat, stirring from time to time, until soft. Add the sugar and cumin and continue cooking until the vegetables are golden brown and slightly caramelized. Season, then transfer to a food processor or blender and blitz to a coarse purée. Chill before serving (it can be stored in a jar in the refrigerator for several days).

To serve, lift the vegetables out of the marinade and place them in dishes or on serving plates. Drizzle with the excess marinade and garnish with coriander leaves. Serve with the croutons and the chilled fennel and cumin jam.

WINE NOTES

An Italian white made with Sauvignon grapes

Oriental Pistou Soup

This French classic is given a new twist with flavours of the Orient.

1 tsp sesame oil
4 tbsp extra virgin olive oil
1 clove garlic, crushed
15g/½oz fresh ginger root,
finely chopped
1 red pepper, cut into 5mm/¼ inch dice
1 green pepper, cut into 5mm/
¼ inch dice
1 courgette, cut into 5mm/¼ inch dice
1 carrot, cut into 5mm/¼ inch dice
1 onion, cut into 5mm/¼ inch dice
1 leek, cut into 5mm/¼ inch dice
salt and freshly ground black pepper
1.5 litres/2½ pints chicken or vegetable
stock (see pages 148, 149)
50g/2oz Chinese egg noodles (optional)
75g/3oz fresh spinach or Chinese
cabbage, coarsely shredded
75g/3oz cooked black soya beans or
ordinary soya beans (cooked weight)

FOR THE ORIENTAL PISTOU
2 tbsp basil leaves
2 tbsp mint leaves
2 tbsp coriander leaves
1 clove garlic, chopped
25g/1oz roasted peanuts
25g/1oz fresh ginger root, finely chopped
a pinch of sugar
about 2 tbsp vegetable oil

Heat the sesame oil and olive oil in a large saucepan with the garlic and ginger. Leave to infuse for 30 seconds before adding the peppers, courgette, carrot, onion and leek. Sweat them over a low heat for 4–5 minutes, then add a little salt and pour in the stock. Bring to the boil, skim off any impurities that rise to the surface and then reduce the heat and simmer for 15–20 minutes, until the vegetables are tender. When they are almost done, add the Chinese noodles, if using, the shredded spinach or cabbage and the soya beans.

Make the oriental pistou by blending all the ingredients together in a food processor or liquidizer, adding enough oil to form a paste. Stir the pistou into the soup just before serving and adjust the seasoning.

N. V.
Suggestion

Add a dice of freshly poached chicken to the soup before serving.

*Oriental Pistou Soup, and Dried Mushroom Soup
with Red Pepper Rouille (page 34)*

Dried Mushroom Soup with Red Pepper Rouille

This is a fairly expensive soup to make because of the dried mushrooms but it has great delicacy and taste.

1 litre/1¾ pints vegetable stock (see page 148)
25g/1oz dried wild mushrooms, such as ceps, trompettes, morels
25g/1oz unsalted butter
½ onion, finely chopped
2 sprigs of thyme
100g/4oz chestnut mushrooms, roughly chopped
4 tbsp white wine
4 tbsp double cream
300ml/½ pint milk
8 baguette croutons (see note opposite)

FOR THE ROUILLE
1 potato
1 small clove garlic, crushed
½ red pepper, blanched and peeled (fresh or tinned)
1 egg yolk
salt and freshly ground black pepper
a little cayenne pepper
3 tbsp extra virgin olive oil

First, bring the vegetable stock to the boil in a saucepan, pour it over the dried mushrooms and leave them to soak for 2 hours (or better still, overnight).

Drain the mushrooms, reserving the liquid, and roughly chop them. Melt the butter in a pan, add the onion and thyme and cook gently for about 4–5 minutes, until the onion is tender. Add the dried mushrooms and the chestnut mushrooms and continue cooking until they start to release their juices.

Pour in the white wine and cook until it is reduced by a third, then stir in the double cream, milk and the liquid from the soaked mushrooms. Bring to the boil, then reduce the heat and simmer, uncovered, for 30–40 minutes.

Meanwhile, prepare the rouille: cook the potato in its skin in a pan of boiling salted water; drain, then when it is cool enough to handle, peel off the skin. Place the garlic and red pepper in a liquidizer and blitz to form a purée. Add the cooked potato, egg yolk, seasoning and cayenne pepper. Then add the olive oil in a thin stream, as if making mayonnaise, until it thickens and forms an emulsion.

Stir half the rouille into the soup and adjust the seasoning to taste. Serve the soup with the remaining rouille and the croutons.

Note: To make baguette croutons, thinly slice a baguette, dip the slices in a little olive oil and toast them under a grill until crisp (or bake them in a moderate oven for 8–10 minutes).

N.V. Suggestion

Add some sautéed lardons of bacon just before serving.

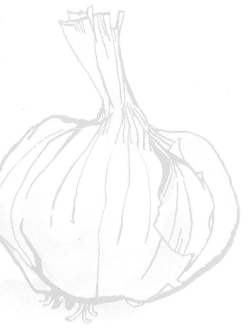

White Cabbage Broth with Fourme d'Ambert Cheese

50g/2oz unsalted butter
250g/9oz white cabbage, cut into
15mm/⅝ inch dice
1 tsp cumin seeds
1 litre/1¾ pints chicken or vegetable
stock (see pages 148, 149)
50g/2oz Fourme d'Ambert cheese (or
other blue cheese)
4 tbsp double cream
salt and freshly ground black pepper
1 tbsp chopped chives (optional)

Melt the butter in a saucepan, add the cabbage, then cover and cook gently without browning for 5–8 minutes. Add the cumin seeds and mix well, then pour on the stock and bring to the boil. Skim off any impurities that rise to the surface and simmer gently for about 30 minutes, until the cabbage is cooked but not mushy.

Pass the Fourme d'Ambert cheese through a fine sieve and blend it with the cream. Add this mixture to the soup and reheat gently but do not let it boil. Adjust the seasoning and serve sprinkled with the chives, if using.

N.V.
Suggestion

Try adding some cleaned fresh oysters with their strained juice to the soup just before serving.

Almond Milk Soup with Jerusalem Artichokes and Nutmeg

Blanching and grinding your own
almonds is a bit laborious but gives
this soup a much better flavour than
using ready-ground ones.

600ml/1 pint milk
250g/9oz almonds, blanched and
ground
600g/1lb 4oz Jerusalem artichokes,
peeled and finely sliced
50g/2oz unsalted butter
600ml/1 pint vegetable stock (see
page 148)
1 bouquet garni
4 tbsp double cream, semi-whipped
salt and freshly ground black pepper
freshly grated nutmeg

Bring the milk to the boil, pour it over the ground almonds and leave to steep overnight. The next day, pass the mixture through a fine strainer to extract as much milk as possible and maximum flavour.

Sauté the artichokes in half the butter for 5 minutes but do not let them colour. Pour in the vegetable stock, add the bouquet garni and cook gently until the artichokes are tender. Purée in a blender, then return the purée to the pan and reheat. Add the almond milk, the semi-whipped cream and the remaining butter to the artichoke purée and pour it back into the blender. Turn the blender on to the highest setting to whip air into the soup (an electric hand blender gives a good result). Season to taste, pour into soup bowls and dust with grated nutmeg. Serve immediately.

N.V.
Suggestion

Add diced chicken to the soup just before serving.

*Cantaloupe Melon Soup with Balsamic Vinegar, and
Butternut Squash and Cannellini Bean Soup (page 38)*

Cantaloupe Melon Soup with Balsamic Vinegar

This refreshing soup makes an ideal starter on a summer's day. I sometimes serve it with a ball of melon sorbet in each portion, usually made with a different variety, such as Ogen, for a good colour contrast. It's very important to choose ripe melons, and they're not difficult to spot if you know what to look for. A ripe melon will feel dense and heavy and the base will yield noticeably when pressed gently. Another means of detection is to smell the top of the melon; it should give off a perfume when ripe. If your melons are a little underripe, leave them at room temperature to ripen rather than in the fridge.

2 medium-sized ripe cantaloupe melons, or other orange-fleshed melons such as Charentais
6 tbsp dry white wine
4 tbsp caster sugar, or more to taste
2 star anise
125ml/4fl oz still mineral water
1 tbsp balsamic vinegar, or more to taste
1 tbsp flaked almonds, toasted
8 mint leaves, chopped

Cut the melons in half and remove the seeds. Cut the flesh away from the skin and reserve half of it for garnish. Dice the remaining flesh and place it in a bowl.

Put the wine, sugar and star anise in a saucepan, bring to the boil and simmer for 2 minutes to form a light syrup. Pour on to the diced melon, add the mineral water and leave to cool.

Remove the star anise from the bowl and discard them, then pour the melon and syrup into a liquidizer or food processor and blitz to a smooth purée. Pass through a fine sieve into a bowl and then stir in the balsamic vinegar. Chill the soup, then test for the balance of acidity and sweetness: you may need to add more sugar if the melon is not sweet enough, or more vinegar to counteract the sweetness.

To garnish the soup, cut the reserved melon into small balls with a melon baller, or alternatively just cut it into small dice. Pour the well-chilled soup into serving bowls and garnish with the melon, toasted almonds and chopped mint. Drizzle with a little balsamic vinegar and serve.

Five-Minute Spinach Soup with Grated Truffle

The truffle is a wonderful but extravagant addition. If you leave it out you will still have a simple, satisfying soup.

450g/1lb fresh young spinach leaves
750ml/1¼ pints chicken or vegetable stock (see pages 148, 149)
6 tbsp double cream
50g/2oz unsalted butter
2 tbsp truffle juice
salt and freshly ground black pepper
freshly grated nutmeg
1 small raw truffle

Pick over the spinach and wash it well several times in clean water to remove any lingering dirt.

Bring the stock to the boil in a saucepan, plunge in the spinach and bring back to the boil. Simmer for 2 minutes, then pour into a blender and blitz to a smooth, thin purée.

Pour the soup back into the pan and bring back to the boil. Remove from the heat, add the cream, butter and truffle juice and whisk well together. Add salt, pepper and nutmeg to taste, and then serve topped with truffle shavings.

Butternut Squash and Cannellini Bean Soup

Serve this hearty rustic soup with some good crusty bread.

150g/5oz dried cannellini beans, soaked
overnight and then drained
4 tbsp vegetable oil
1 onion, chopped
1 clove garlic, finely chopped
1 celery stick, chopped
½ tsp ground cumin
1 large butternut squash, peeled and cut
into 1cm/½ inch dice
5 tbsp Tomato Concassée (see page 151)
1 tbsp chopped rosemary
salt and freshly ground black pepper

Put the cannellini beans into a saucepan, cover with water and bring to the boil. Reduce the heat and simmer for 1–1½ hours or until tender, then drain. Reserve the cooking water.

Heat the oil in a large saucepan, add the onion, garlic, celery and cumin and cook for about 5 minutes until the vegetables are tender. Add the diced butternut squash and mix in well. Pour in the reserved cooking liquid from the beans, bring to the boil, then reduce the heat and cook gently for 10–15 minutes, until the squash is soft and tender. Remove half the cooked squash from the pan and set aside. Add the tomato concassée to the pan and cook for a further 10 minutes.

Pour the soup into a food processor and blitz to a smooth purée, then pour it into a clean pan. Bring it back to the boil and add the rosemary, cooked cannellini beans and reserved butternut squash. Heat through, then season to taste and serve.

Grilled Aubergine Soup with Coriander Chutney

2 aubergines, peeled and cut into slices
5mm/¼ inch thick
olive oil for brushing
50g/2oz unsalted butter
½ onion, roughly chopped
1 clove garlic, crushed
½ leek, roughly chopped
1 tbsp Home-made Curry Powder (see
page 154)
½ tsp ground coriander
¼ tsp ground cumin
1 litre/1¾ pints chicken or vegetable
stock (see pages 148, 149)
2 tbsp yogurt
salt and freshly ground black pepper

FOR THE CORIANDER CHUTNEY
50g/2oz coriander, chopped
2 small green chillies, deseeded and
chopped
3 tbsp lemon juice
¼ onion, chopped

Brush the aubergine slices with a little olive oil, then place them under a hot grill and cook until brown and tender. Heat the butter in a pan, add the onion, garlic and leek and sweat for 5 minutes. Add the grilled aubergine slices and the spices, cover and cook for 5 minutes over a very low heat. Pour in the stock, bring to the boil and cook for a further 10 minutes. Meanwhile, make the coriander chutney by briefly processing all the ingredients together in a liquidizer or food processor until it forms a slightly chunky consistency. The chutney will keep well in a storage jar in the fridge for 4–5 days.

Pour the soup into a blender and blitz until smooth. Return it to a clean pan, heat gently, then add the yogurt and adjust the seasoning. Pour into serving bowls and top with a spoonful of the chutney.

Lemon Chick Pea Soup with Olive Oil

The classic Middle Eastern dip hummus is transformed here into a delicious soup.

350g/13oz dried chick peas, soaked overnight and then drained
1 onion, roughly chopped
2 cloves garlic, crushed
8 basil leaves
1.5 litres/2½ pints chicken or vegetable stock (see pages 148, 149)
4 tbsp tahini
2 tbsp lemon juice
7 tbsp extra virgin olive oil
salt and freshly ground black pepper
cayenne pepper
2 eggs, hard-boiled
1 tbsp chopped parsley

Place the chick peas, onion, garlic and basil in a pot, pour in the stock and bring to the boil. Reduce the heat and simmer for about an hour or until the chick peas are tender, topping up with a little more stock or water if necessary.

When the chick peas are cooked, add the tahini, then transfer the mixture to a blender and blitz to a fine purée. Pour into a bowl and stir in the lemon juice and 6 tablespoons of the olive oil. Season, adding cayenne pepper to taste, and thin the soup with a little stock or water if necessary. Chill the soup thoroughly.

To serve, chop the eggs very finely or pass them through a sieve, and mix with the parsley. Drizzle the remaining olive oil over the soup then sprinkle on the egg and parsley mixture.

> ### N.V.
> ### Suggestion
>
> Garnish the soup with small cubes of tuna marinated in olive oil and lemon juice.

Honey-Roasted Parsnip Soup

This soup can be garnished with some diced bread croutons, fried in butter until golden.

25g/1oz unsalted butter
500g/1lb 2oz parsnips, roughly chopped
½ onion, roughly chopped
1 carrot, roughly chopped
1 small clove garlic, roughly chopped
1 tsp thyme leaves
1 small bay leaf
1 tbsp clear honey
1 litre/1¾ pints chicken or vegetable
stock (see pages 148, 149)
6 tbsp dry cider
4 tbsp double cream

Preheat the oven to 220°C (425°F, Gas Mark 7). Heat the butter in an ovenproof casserole dish, add the parsnips and roast in the oven for about 25–30 minutes, until golden brown. Add the onion, carrot and garlic and continue cooking for a further 10 minutes, then mix in the herbs and honey. Cook for about 10 minutes, until the vegetables have caramelized.

Now remove the dish from the oven, add the stock and bring to the boil on top of the stove. Reduce the heat and simmer for 10 minutes. Add the cider then pour the soup into a blender and purée until smooth. Strain through a fine strainer, bring back to the boil, then remove from the heat, swirl in the cream and serve.

Chilled Turnip Soup Perfumed with Vanilla

This may also be served hot and is equally successful using potatoes instead of turnips. Don't be tempted to use vanilla essence or extract instead of the vanilla pod as the result just isn't the same.

½ vanilla pod
125ml/4fl oz milk
25g/1oz unsalted butter
50g/2oz shallots, roughly chopped
250g/9oz young turnips, chopped
100g/4oz leek, white part only,
roughly chopped
1 litre/1¾ pints vegetable stock
(see page 148)
250ml/8fl oz single cream
salt and freshly ground black pepper
1 tbsp chervil leaves

Split the vanilla pod in half lengthways and scrape off the seeds with a knife. Put both the seeds and the pod in a pan with the milk and bring slowly to the boil. Take off the heat and remove the pod.

Melt the butter in a heavy-based pan and add the shallots. Sweat them gently until tender but not browned, then add the turnips and leek and cook for a few minutes. Pour in the vegetable stock, followed by the vanilla-infused milk and half the cream. Cook gently over a low heat until all the vegetables are soft.

Pour the soup into a blender and liquidize it to a fine purée. Pass it through a fine strainer to remove any remaining fibres and then pour it into a clean bowl. Place in the refrigerator until thoroughly chilled.

To serve, season to taste and stir in the remaining cream, then garnish with the chervil leaves. Serve the soup well chilled.

Velouté of Cauliflower and Walnut with Soy Milk

I like to use soy milk in this recipe because it combines well with the earthy flavour of the walnuts but any type of milk may be substituted.

400g/14oz cauliflower, cut into smallish florets
50g/2oz walnuts
25g/1oz unsalted butter
750ml/1¼ pints chicken or vegetable stock (see pages 148, 149)
250ml/8fl oz soy milk
2 tbsp chopped chervil or parsley
salt and freshly ground black pepper
1 egg yolk
4 tbsp crème fraîche

Cook about 100g/4oz of the cauliflower florets in boiling salted water until just tender, then drain and set aside for garnish.

Put the walnuts in a small pan of boiling water and simmer for 3–4 minutes, then drain and rinse under cold water (this makes them easier to peel). Peel off the brown papery skins and chop the walnuts roughly. Heat the butter in a pan, add the walnuts and sauté until lightly browned. Remove 1 tablespoon of walnuts from the pan and set aside for garnish. Add the remaining cauliflower to the pan and cook for a few more minutes. Pour in the stock, bring to the boil and simmer until the cauliflower is tender. Add the soy milk and chervil or parsley, then pour into a blender or food processor and blitz until smooth. Season to taste.

Mix the egg yolk and crème fraîche together in a large bowl and then pour the soup over them. Return it to a pan and cook very gently for 30 seconds or until the mixture thickens slightly. Do not let it boil or it will curdle.

Pour the soup into bowls, sprinkle with the reserved walnuts and cauliflower florets and then serve.

Salads and Light Dishes

In this chapter I have put together a tasty selection of dishes for the occasion when something light fits the bill perfectly.

To many people the word salad conjures up visions of limp lettuce with tomatoes and cucumber, but why should it? Take the wealth of new salad leaves, fresh garden herbs and other wonderful ingredients now at our disposal and combine them with a little imagination to create wonderful salads. I have also included some Salad Do's and Don'ts and tips on how to get the best results.

As you will see, the recipes vary in complexity and composition, some light, some more substantial and some equally suitable to serve as a light main course.

Wild Rice Couscous Salad

The rice is finely chopped to resemble small dark grains of couscous, hence the name. I sometimes fill roasted peppers with the salad and serve with young spinach leaves and feta cheese.

15g/5oz wild rice, soaked overnight and
then drained
salt and freshly ground black pepper
50g/2oz unsalted butter
1 onion, finely diced
1 clove garlic, crushed
1 green pepper, finely diced
1 tsp cumin seeds
100g/4oz chick peas, cooked
50g/2oz raisins, soaked in warm water
until plump

25g/1oz pine kernels
6 spring onions, shredded
1 apple, peeled, cored and finely diced
a little cinnamon

FOR THE DRESSING
6 tbsp extra virgin olive oil
2 tbsp white wine vinegar
1 tbsp balsamic vinegar
½ tbsp chopped mint

Put the wild rice in a saucepan, cover with water, add a little salt and simmer for about 20–30 minutes, until tender (if the rice has not been soaked it will take longer to cook). Drain in a colander and leave to cool.

Heat the butter in a pan, add the onion, garlic, green pepper, cumin and cooked chick peas and cook for a few minutes until the onion is tender. Add the raisins and pine kernels and raise the heat to colour the pine kernels slightly.

Put the cooked rice on a chopping board and chop it with a large knife until it is very fine and resembles small beads. Add the rice to the pan, mix well and season to taste.

Mix together all the ingredients for the dressing and stir into the pan with the spring onions and apple. Adjust the seasoning, adding salt, pepper and cinnamon to taste, and then serve.

Fennel Salad with Beetroot, Roquefort and Paprika Cashews

1 tbsp extra virgin olive oil
2 tbsp cashew nuts
a little paprika
2 large fennel bulbs, thinly sliced
2 cooked beetroots (not in vinegar),
peeled and sliced

FOR THE DRESSING
65g/2½oz Roquefort cheese
6 tbsp double cream
2 tbsp sherry vinegar or white
wine vinegar
3 tbsp extra virgin olive oil
salt and freshly ground black pepper

Heat the olive oil, add the cashews, season with a little paprika and fry for 1 minute. Remove from the heat and leave to cool.

To make the dressing, purée the Roquefort cheese in a liquidizer or put it in a bowl and mash it with a fork until smooth. Add the cream, vinegar, oil and seasoning and mix well. Toss the sliced fennel in the dressing and adjust the seasoning to taste. Transfer to a serving bowl, garnish with the beetroot slices and paprika cashews and then serve.

WINE NOTES

A fresh, light and fruity New Zealand Sauvignon

Pasta Caesar Salad with Blue Cheese

Add some thinly sliced button mushrooms and sun-dried tomatoes for an occasional variation.

175g/6oz penne
salt and freshly ground black pepper
50g/2oz Gorgonzola cheese
2 tbsp double cream
2 slices of white bread, toasted
4 Little Gem lettuces or 2 large Cos lettuces
1 tbsp freshly grated Parmesan cheese

FOR THE DRESSING
2 cloves garlic, crushed
4 tbsp extra virgin olive oil
4 tbsp vegetable oil
1 egg
1 tbsp red wine vinegar
juice of ½ lemon
1 tsp Dijon mustard
a drop of Worcestershire sauce
a drop of Tabasco sauce

First prepare the dressing by blending all the ingredients together with a whisk or in a liquidizer.

Cook the pasta in plenty of boiling water until *al dente*, drain it well and dry in a cloth. Leave to cool for 4–5 minutes, then place in a bowl. Mix in the dressing, season and leave at room temperature for about 10 minutes so the pasta can absorb the flavours.

Blend the Gorgonzola cheese with the cream, then spread it over the toast and place under a hot grill until golden brown. Cut off the crusts and cut the toast into neat fingers or dice.

Wash and dry the lettuce, put it in a serving bowl or on individual plates and put the pasta and dressing on top. Scatter the cheese croutons over the pasta, then sprinkle on the Parmesan and serve.

N.V. Suggestion

Add thinly sliced grilled chicken breast or, for a classic Caesar salad flavour, diced anchovy fillets.

WINE NOTES

A fairly oaky Australian Chardonnay

*T*ricolour Salad with Passion Fruit Vinaigrette,
and Fattoush

Tricolour Salad with Passion Fruit Vinaigrette

2 heads of white chicory
1 head of radicchio
1 bunch of watercress
1 pink grapefruit
12 asparagus spears, trimmed
and peeled
1 avocado
1 tsp poppy seeds, lightly toasted

FOR THE PASSION FRUIT VINAIGRETTE
juice of 2 passion fruit, strained
1 tbsp orange juice
½ tbsp champagne vinegar
6 tbsp groundnut oil or extra virgin
olive oil
salt and freshly ground black pepper

Trim the chicory, radicchio and watercress, removing any rough outer leaves from the chicory and radicchio and separating the remaining leaves. Wash the leaves, spin them in a salad spinner to extract any clinging water and dry them in a cloth. Shred the radicchio into long strands.

Segment the pink grapefruit (see note below), put the segments in a bowl and set aside. Cook the asparagus in boiling salted water for 3–4 minutes, refresh it in cold water, then drain and dry. Cut the spears into 5cm/2 inch lengths.

Prepare the vinaigrette by mixing all the ingredients together in a bowl, adding seasoning to taste.

Just before serving, peel and stone the avocado and cut the flesh into slices or large dice. Arrange the salad leaves in a large serving bowl or in individual dishes and scatter the avocado, asparagus and grapefruit over them. Season with a touch of cracked black pepper and then drizzle over the passion fruit vinaigrette. Garnish the salad with the toasted poppy seeds and serve immediately.

Note: To segment citrus fruits, cut a small slice off each end of the fruit and then, working from the top to the bottom, cut off the skin and white pith, carefully following the curve of the fruit. Now hold the fruit in your hand over a bowl to catch the juice and, using a small paring knife, cut between each membrane to release the individual segments.

Fattoush (Syrian Bread Salad)

1 cucumber, peeled, deseeded and cut
into 1cm/½ inch dice
salt and freshly ground black pepper
6 tbsp extra virgin olive oil
3 pitta breads or 5 slices of white bread,
cut into strips 1cm/½ inch wide
2 cloves garlic, crushed
juice of 1 lemon
2 tbsp roughly chopped flat-leaf parsley
2 tbsp roughly chopped coriander leaves
2 tbsp roughly chopped mint

1 red onion, cut into 1cm/½ inch dice
5 ripe tomatoes, peeled, deseeded and cut
into 1cm/½ inch dice
2 small green peppers, cut into 1cm/
½ inch dice

Place the diced cucumber in a colander, sprinkle with salt and leave to drain for 20 minutes.

Heat 2 tablespoons of the oil in a frying pan and fry the bread until it is golden brown. Drain on kitchen paper to remove any excess oil.

In a large bowl mix together the garlic, lemon juice, the remaining olive oil and the herbs to make a dressing. Add the diced vegetables and toss well to coat with the dressing. Season with salt and pepper, garnish with the strips of fried bread and serve immediately.

Warm Mixed Bean Salad with Grilled Radicchio, Red Onion and Thyme

*150g/5oz haricot beans, soaked
overnight and then drained
1 bay leaf
1 clove garlic, peeled and halved
200g/7oz French beans
100g/4oz fresh broad beans, shelled
2 heads of radicchio, cut into quarters
2 tbsp extra virgin olive oil
1 red onion, finely chopped
1 tbsp thyme leaves
salt and freshly ground black pepper
150ml/¼ pint Basic Vinaigrette (see
page 51)
50g/2oz flat-leaf parsley, chopped*

Put the haricot beans in a saucepan, cover with cold water, add the bay leaf and the garlic and bring to the boil. Reduce the heat and simmer for 1–1½ hours, until the beans are tender. Drain them in a colander and set aside.

Cook the French beans and broad beans in two separate pans of boiling water until just tender but still slightly firm; drain them in a colander and refresh under cold running water.

Brush the radicchio quarters with half the olive oil and cook on a barbecue or under a preheated hot grill until lightly charred. Heat the remaining olive oil in a pan, add the red onion, thyme leaves and all the cooked beans and season lightly. Pour in the vinaigrette and mix well. After about 2 minutes, when all the ingredients are warmed through, remove from the heat and stir in the parsley.

Arrange the grilled raddichio on a serving dish and spoon the warm bean salad over and around it. Serve at once.

N. V.
Suggestion

Top the salad with thin slices of freshly grilled duck breast and a few toasted croutons.

Cypriot Hot Potato Salad with Cracked Coriander Seeds

I like to serve these potatoes on a little wilted spinach that has been sautéed in olive oil with a touch of garlic.

*4 tbsp extra virgin olive oil
450g/1lb new potatoes (preferably
Cyprus or Jersey), halved
salt and freshly ground black pepper
125ml/4fl oz dry white wine
2 tbsp coriander seeds, lightly crushed*

Preheat the oven to 200°C (400°F, Gas Mark 6). Heat the olive oil in an ovenproof casserole, add the potatoes and fry until golden all over. Season lightly and place in the oven for 10 minutes until almost cooked.

Remove the dish from the oven and place over a medium heat. Add the wine and cracked coriander seeds, cover and simmer for 5–8 minutes until the liquid has evaporated. Season to taste and serve.

WINE NOTES

A New Zealand unoaked Chardonnay

*W*arm Mixed Bean Salad with Grilled Radicchio, Red Onion and Thyme,
and New Mediterranean Salad (page 50)

New Mediterranean Salad

4 heads of Little Gem lettuce, leaves
separated
4 plum tomatoes, sliced or cut
into quarters
½ cucumber, peeled, cut into half
lengthways and deseeded, then cut into
1cm/½ inch slices
1 red onion, cut into thin rings
1 red pepper, cut into thin strips
1 green pepper, cut into thin strips
a little extra virgin olive oil
150g/5oz feta or haloumi cheese
1 tbsp Piquant Lemon Relish (see
page 154)
a few rocket leaves, to garnish (optional)

FOR THE DRESSING
6 tbsp extra virgin olive oil
1 tbsp white wine vinegar or lemon juice
1 clove garlic, crushed
10 black olives, rinsed, stoned and finely
sliced
1 tsp capers, rinsed and chopped
1 tbsp chopped oregano or parsley
salt and freshly ground black pepper

For the dressing, mix together the oil and vinegar or lemon juice, then add the garlic, olives and capers and leave to marinate for 30 minutes. Add the oregano or parsley and season.

Put the lettuce, tomatoes, cucumber, onion and peppers into a bowl and toss with a little olive oil to coat the leaves. Arrange attractively on serving plates.

Cut the cheese into eight 8mm/⅜ inch slices, brush with a little olive oil and place under a hot grill or on a barbecue until browned. Put 2 slices on each salad, pour over the olive dressing, trickling a little more around the edges of the salad. Scatter the lemon relish over the cheese, garnish with rocket, if using, and serve.

N.V.
Suggestion

Replace the cheese with freshly grilled or fried tuna or sardines.

Aubergine Salad

800g/1¾lb aubergines
salt and freshly ground black pepper
150ml/¼ pint extra virgin olive oil
½ tsp Home-made Curry Powder
(see page 154)
1 tsp ground cumin
1 tsp turmeric
1 tsp good-quality red wine vinegar,
such as Cabernet Sauvignon
1 clove garlic, crushed
125ml/4fl oz yogurt
a pinch of cinnamon
50g/2oz raisins, soaked in warm water
until plump
2 tbsp chopped walnuts
freshly grated nutmeg
½ tsp black mustard seeds (optional)

Peel the aubergines, cut the skin into fine shreds and set aside. Cut the aubergines into 1cm/½ inch dice, salt them and leave in a colander for 45 minutes to drain. Rinse, drain and dry them well.

Heat 2 tablespoons of the oil in a frying pan, add half the curry powder, cumin and turmeric and fry half the aubergine until softened and lightly golden. Repeat with the remaining aubergine and spices and 2 more tablespoons of oil. Place the aubergine in a dish and cool slightly.

Mix together the vinegar, garlic, yogurt, cinnamon, raisins, walnuts and nutmeg and stir into the aubergine. Heat the remaining olive oil in a pan and fry the shredded aubergine skin until crispy, then drain it on paper towels and salt it. If using the mustard seeds, sprinkle them over the salad, then garnish with the fried aubergine skin. Serve at room temperature.

Ultimate Tossed Green Salad

There was a time earlier in my career when I thought salads were strictly for dieters. However, I have come to realize that even a simple green salad must be treated with respect and, as with any other dish, it is vital to use the best-quality ingredients. Always choose salad leaves that are at their best; I tend to discard the lollo rosso and batavia varieties, which have more to do with fashion than with taste. My favourite leaves are listed below.

250g/9oz mixed green salad leaves, such as mâche, Cos, Little Gem, rocket, frisée or young spinach
1 small clove garlic, halved
1 shallot, finely chopped
½ tsp herb mustard
2 tbsp champagne vinegar
salt
125ml/4fl oz extra virgin olive oil
50g/2oz mixed herbs, such as basil, tarragon, chervil, flat-leaf parsley or mint

Wash the salad leaves and dry them well. Rub the inside of a salad bowl liberally with the garlic. In a separate bowl, mix together the chopped shallot, the herb mustard, vinegar and a little salt. Whisk in the oil to form an emulsion and adjust the seasoning.

Toss the leaves with the herbs in the salad bowl and carefully add the dressing. Toss together until all the leaves are lightly coated with the dressing, adjust the seasoning again and serve immediately.

SALAD DO'S AND DON'TS:
1. Always select fresh crisp salad leaves.
2. Tightly packed leaves such as raddichio or Cos need to be washed well, as they often harbour dirt. I always wash them in lightly salted water, but never leave them to soak – just dunk them in briefly.
3. Make sure the washed leaves are thoroughly dry before you add the dressing. A salad spinner is the best way to remove excess water.
4. Always dress your salad at the last possible moment before serving.
5. Never add too much dressing, as the leaves absorb it quickly and will become saturated.

Basic Vinaigrette

Every chef will tell you his or her own formula for vinaigrette but really the oil-to-vinegar ratio should be adjusted according to the ingredients in the salad. We all have a different tolerance of acidity levels, so personal preference has a part to play, too. I find this vinaigrette ideal for many purposes, but some people may not like it quite so mustardy. I love to add herbs, such as parsley, tarragon and chervil.

3 tbsp good-quality red wine vinegar, such as Cabernet Sauvignon
1–1½ tsp Dijon mustard
1 small clove garlic, crushed
5 tbsp extra virgin olive oil
5 tbsp groundnut or vegetable oil
salt and freshly ground black pepper

Mix all the ingredients together in a bowl and season to taste.

Basic Mayonnaise

Mayonnaise is one of the most underrated sauces in the culinary repertoire. Although it is relatively simple to make there are certain guidelines that should be adhered to for success (see opposite).

2 egg yolks
2 tsp cider vinegar or white wine vinegar
1 tsp Dijon mustard
salt and freshly ground black pepper
250ml/8fl oz extra virgin olive oil

Place the egg yolks in a bowl with the vinegar, mustard, salt and pepper and whisk together with a balloon whisk or electric beater. Then add the oil in a very slow trickle, beating constantly. To ensure the oil dribbles out a little at a time, use a spouted jug or a bottle with a small hole cut in the lid. When all the oil has been added you should have a thick glossy emulsion that clings to the whisk.

If the mayonnaise is not to be used immediately, add a little boiling water to help prevent it curdling.

MAYONNAISE WITH A SPICY TOUCH

Add 1 teaspoon of Home-made Curry Powder (see page 154), paprika or aniseed to the egg yolks with the vinegar and mustard.

CITRUS MAYONNAISE

Add 1 tablespoon of grated lemon or orange zest plus 1 tablespoon of juice.

RED WINE MAYONNAISE

Put 150ml/¼ pint red wine in a pan and boil until it is reduced to about 2 tablespoons. Add this to the egg yolks with a little pinch of sugar and substitute red wine vinegar for the cider or white wine vinegar.

NIÇOISE MAYONNAISE

Stir 2 teaspoons of Black Olive Tapenade (see page 153) into the finished mayonnaise.

FRESH VEGETABLE OR HERB MAYONNAISE

Stir about 100g/4oz fresh vegetable or herb purée into the mayonnaise.

MAYONNAISE DO'S AND DON'TS:

1. Bring all the ingredients to room temperature before you start.
2. Make sure that the mixing bowl is thoroughly clean and dry.
3. Always add the oil to the eggs very slowly to form a good emulsion (the maximum oil one egg yolk can absorb is about 150ml/¼ pint).
4. If by some chance the mayonnaise does begin to curdle it can quite easily be saved by whisking in 2 tablespoons of boiling water. If this doesn't work, beat together an egg yolk and 1 tablespoon of boiling water in a clean bowl, then gradually add the curdled mayonnaise a little at a time, beating well between each addition.
5. Mayonnaise will keep well in a refrigerator for up to one week but always bring it back to room temperature before serving for the best results.

Mayonnaise with no Eggs

Many people prefer to avoid raw eggs nowadays because of the salmonella scare. Although there should be no health risk if you use free-range eggs from a reputable source, not everyone can check the reliability of their supplier. Here is an egg-free mayonnaise recipe which can be used in the same way as classic mayonnaise and will keep in the fridge for up to a week.

4 tbsp unsweetened condensed milk
2 tsp Dijon mustard
salt and freshly ground black pepper
125ml/4fl oz extra virgin olive oil
2 tbsp cider vinegar or white wine vinegar
a squeeze of lemon juice
2 tsp yogurt

Place the condensed milk, mustard, salt and pepper in a bowl and whisk in the oil a little at a time. When all the oil has been incorporated, add the vinegar, which will thicken the sauce immediately (this is due to the acid from the vinegar reacting with the milk). Stir in a squeeze of lemon juice and the yogurt and adjust the seasoning to taste.

My Aioli Sauce – Baked Garlic Mayonnaise

3–4 cloves garlic, unpeeled
2 egg yolks
juice of ½ lemon
salt and freshly ground black pepper
125ml/4fl oz groundnut oil
125ml/4fl oz extra virgin olive oil

Preheat the oven to 180°C (350°F, Gas Mark 4). Wrap the garlic cloves loosely in aluminium foil, place on a baking tray and bake for 25 minutes or until very tender. Peel off the skin and pass the garlic through a fine sieve to make a purée.

Place the egg yolks, garlic, lemon juice and seasoning in a bowl and proceed as for Basic Mayonnaise.

Sweetcorn Clafoutis with Cherry Tomatoes, Peas and Baked Egg, and Middle Eastern Omelette

54

Sweetcorn Clafoutis with Cherry Tomatoes, Peas and Baked Egg

*100g/4oz fresh or canned sweetcorn
kernels
250ml/8fl oz milk
8 eggs
25g/1oz plain flour
125ml/4fl oz double cream
salt and freshly ground black pepper
25g/1oz unsalted butter
12 cherry tomatoes
50g/2oz young peas, cooked
a little Pecorino cheese, grated
4 tbsp Genoese Pesto Sauce (see
page 152)*

Preheat the oven to 180°C (350°F, Gas Mark 4). Put the sweetcorn and milk in a saucepan and bring to the boil. Reduce the heat and cook for about 8–10 minutes, until the sweetcorn is very tender. Drain, reserving the milk.

When the milk is cool, put it in a food processor or liquidizer with half the sweetcorn and blitz to a purée. In a bowl, whisk together 4 of the eggs, gradually whisk in the flour and finally add the sweetcorn purée and the cream to make a batter. Season to taste.

Heat the butter in a pan, add the cherry tomatoes and cook gently for 1 minute before adding the remaining sweetcorn and the peas. Season to taste with salt and pepper.

Lightly butter 4 individual ovenproof dishes and arrange the tomatoes, sweetcorn and peas around the edge of each one, leaving a space in the centre of each dish. Carefully pour in the sweetcorn batter and bake in the preheated oven for 6 minutes. Crack an egg into the centre of each dish, sprinkle with Pecorino cheese and cook for a further 4–6 minutes, until the eggs are set. Remove from the oven, drizzle a spoonful of pesto around each egg and serve immediately.

Middle Eastern Omelette

This omelette mixture is cooked in a terrine dish but you could also use an ovenproof frying pan and cut the omelette into wedges to serve. Fresh tomato sauce makes a good alternative to the crème fraîche.

*50g/2oz bunch of parsley
75g/3oz bunch of coriander
25g/1oz bunch of mint
25g/1oz chives, chopped
4 spring onions, chopped
75g/3oz spinach or Swiss chard, cooked,
well drained and coarsely chopped
a pinch of paprika*

*salt and freshly ground black pepper
8 eggs
¼ tsp saffron strands (optional)
50g/2oz unsalted butter
2 tbsp crème fraîche
1 red chilli, deseeded and finely sliced*

Preheat the oven to 160°C (325°F, Gas Mark 3). Strip the leaves from the parsley, coriander and mint and chop them finely. Put them in a bowl with the chives, spring onions and cooked spinach or Swiss chard, add the paprika and a little salt and pepper and mix well together.

Beat the eggs in a separate bowl until frothy, add the saffron if using, mix well and pour over the greens.

Melt the butter in a small pan and pour it into a 20cm/8 inch terrine dish or loaf tin; pour in the omelette mixture and then bake in the oven for about 30 minutes or until the omelette is set and lightly golden on top.

Leave the omelette to cool, then turn it out of the terrine and serve cut into slices or wedges, garnished with the crème fraîche and chilli.

Soufflé Omelette with Tapenade and Cream Cheese

4 eggs, separated
5 basil leaves, chopped
salt and freshly ground black pepper
2 tbsp extra virgin olive oil or clarified
butter (see page 151)
1 tbsp pine kernels, toasted (optional)
2 tbsp cream cheese
2 tbsp Black Olive Tapenade, warmed
(see page 153)
½ tbsp finely grated Parmesan cheese

SERVES 2

Beat the egg yolks in a bowl until light and airy. Add the basil and season with salt and pepper. In a separate bowl, beat the egg whites until they form stiff peaks; carefully fold them into the beaten yolks.

Put a tablespoon of the oil or clarified butter in a heavy-based 20cm/ 8 inch omelette pan over a fairly high heat. Scatter over half the pine kernels, if using, and add half the omelette mixture. Lightly smooth the top to ensure a good shape, then cook until the omelette is just beginning to set but is still soft on top.

Place a spoonful of cream cheese on the omelette and gently spread it over the surface, then add a spoonful of warmed tapenade. Fold the omelette in half to enclose the filling, then turn it out on to a serving plate, dust with Parmesan cheese and serve immediately. Make the second omelette in the same way.

Gruyère Cheesecakes with Pesto

These delicate warm cheesecakes are delicious and simple to make.

½ red pepper, very finely diced
150ml/¼ pint milk
50g/2oz unsalted butter
65g/2½oz self-raising flour
3 eggs
2 egg yolks
250ml/8fl oz single or whipping cream
50g/2oz cream cheese
50g/2oz Gruyère cheese, grated
salt and freshly ground black pepper
freshly grated nutmeg
4 tbsp Genoese Pesto Sauce (see
page 152)
125ml/4fl oz Grilled Tomato Sauce
(see page 152)

Preheat the oven to 160°C (325°F, Gas Mark 3). Cook the diced red pepper in a little boiling water until soft, then drain.

Put the milk and butter in a pan and bring to the boil. Gradually rain in the flour and beat it well, then reduce the heat to low and continue beating for 1–2 minutes to cook the flour. Mix the eggs, yolks and cream together, add to the pan and mix well. Finally, add the cream cheese, Gruyère and cooked pepper and season with salt, pepper and nutmeg.

Butter 4 individual soufflé dishes, 200–250ml/7–8fl oz in capacity, and fill them with the cheesecake mixture. Place them in a shallow ovenproof dish or roasting tin and pour in enough boiling water to come a third of the way up the outside of the dishes. Bake in the preheated oven for about 10–12 minutes, until lightly set and golden.

Turn out the cheesecakes on to serving plates and top each one with a spoonful of pesto, then pour the grilled tomato sauce around them. Serve immediately.

N. V. Suffered
N. V. Suggestion

Serve with crispy fried slices of prosciutto.

*T*omato and Courgette Tians with Fennel Soubise

A soubise is usually a purée of cooked onion or shallots thickened with rice. Here the rice is omitted and fennel is added to the onion. You could include thin layers of cooked pasta with the vegetables for a lasagne-style alternative.

50g/2oz unsalted butter
½ onion, thinly sliced
2 fennel bulbs, thinly sliced
1 tsp chopped dill
½ tsp Dijon mustard
5 tbsp extra virgin olive oil
4 courgettes, cut into slices 5mm/
¼ inch thick
salt and freshly ground black pepper
4 ripe but firm plum tomatoes, cut into slices 5mm/¼ inch thick
200ml/7fl oz Basic White Sauce (see page 149)
75g/3oz soft goat's cheese

WINE NOTES

An Alsace Riesling or Anjou Rosé

*P*reheat the oven to 200°C (400°F, Gas Mark 6). Heat the butter in a pan and add the onion and fennel. Cook over a gentle heat for 15–20 minutes until golden and tender, then leave to cool. Transfer the mixture to a food processor and blitz to form a coarse purée; alternatively chop it very finely with a knife. Add the dill and mustard and set aside.

Heat the olive oil in a frying pan, add the courgettes and cook for 4–5 minutes, until golden. Remove from the heat and season to taste.

Take four 8–10cm/3–4 inch metal baking rings (if you don't have any you could use individual gratin dishes or one large baking dish), butter them well and place on a baking sheet. Arrange some of the courgettes in the base of each ring, then add a layer of tomato slices. Continue layering them in this way until the rings are half full, then add a layer of fennel purée about 5mm/¼ inch thick. Top with more courgette and tomato layers until the rings are full. Push the vegetables down into the ring to compress them.

Gently reheat the white sauce if necessary, mix in the goat's cheese and season to taste. Coat the top of each tian with the sauce and then bake in the preheated oven for 10–12 minutes until golden.

Put the tians on individual serving plates, carefully remove the rings and serve immediately.

Artichokes Mimosa in Tarragon Jelly

If baby artichokes are not available you can use larger globe artichokes or even Jerusalem artichokes – or why not try a mixture of both?

24 baby purple Breton artichokes
2 tbsp extra virgin olive oil
4 shallots, chopped
150ml/¼ pint dry white wine
1 litre/1¾ pints chicken or vegetable
stock (see pages 148, 149)
salt and freshly ground black pepper
1 small bunch of tarragon, stalks and
leaves separated
1 small bay leaf
5 gelatine leaves (or vegetarian
equivalent)
3 eggs, hard-boiled, whites and yolks
separated and chopped
1 tsp green peppercorns, rinsed
and drained
4 tomatoes, peeled, deseeded and
finely diced

FOR THE BEETROOT VINAIGRETTE
2 raw beetroot
6 tbsp sherry vinegar or red wine
vinegar
½ tsp Dijon mustard
200ml/7fl oz groundnut or vegetable oil

SERVES 10–12

Preheat the oven to 180°C (350°F, Gas Mark 4). Prepare the artichokes by removing the stalks and cutting 1cm/½ inch off the tops of the leaves. As the artichokes are very young and tender no other preparation is required.

Heat the oil in an ovenproof casserole and add the shallots. Sweat gently until tender, then add the artichokes and the white wine and bring to the boil. Boil for 1 minute and then add the stock. Season lightly and add the tarragon stalks and the bay leaf. Return to the boil, cover with a lid or aluminium foil and transfer the dish to the preheated oven. Bake for 10–15 minutes, until the artichokes are tender, then remove them from the cooking liquid and set aside. Cool the liquid slightly, then skim off any oil or impurities from the surface with a ladle.

Put the gelatine in a small bowl, cover it with water and leave for a few minutes until soft, then stir it into the warm liquid and strain through a fine sieve. Chop the tarragon leaves and add them to the liquid. Leave until it is beginning to set, then pour a little of the tarragon jelly into a loaf tin or terrine 20cm/8 inches long. Sprinkle with some of the chopped egg white and yolk, a few peppercorns, diced tomato and then some of the artichokes. Top up with a little of the jelly. Repeat this process to fill the terrine, packing it very tightly, until all the

ingredients are used up. Place in the refrigerator to set for at least 8 or up to 24 hours.

Meanwhile, make the beetroot vinaigrette. Extract the juice from the beetroot (see page 146). Place the juice in a pan and bring to the boil. Skim off any impurities that rise to the surface then reduce the heat to a simmer. Add the vinegar and continue cooking until it is reduced by half its original volume and becomes syrupy in appearance. Allow to cool, then add the mustard. Whisk in the oil to form a vinaigrette and season to taste.

To serve, dip the terrine in hot water for 5–10 seconds and turn it out on to a plate. Cut it into slices 1cm/½ inch thick and serve with the beetroot vinaigrette.

WINE NOTES

A Pinot Blanc, Sylvaner, or other light, not too spicy Alsace white

*A*rtichokes Mimosa in Tarragon Jelly, and Courgette Tarts with
Walnut Frangipane and Thyme Butter (page 60)

Courgette Tarts with Walnut Frangipane and Thyme Butter

Served with a salad dressed with balsamic vinaigrette (with truffle juice if you have some), these tarts make an ideal light lunch dish or appetizer. You can vary the filling in all sorts of ways: try pine kernel frangipane topped with sliced tomatoes or peppers, or chestnut topped with aubergine slices.

90g/3½oz unsalted butter
4 sheets of filo pastry
2 shallots, finely chopped
1 clove garlic, crushed
1 egg
40g/1½oz brioche crumbs or white breadcrumbs
65g/2½oz walnuts, ground
2 tbsp double cream
salt and freshly ground black pepper
2 green courgettes, cut into slices 8mm/⅜ inch thick
2 yellow courgettes, cut into slices 8mm/⅜ inch thick
1 tbsp thyme leaves
a little celery salt (optional)

Preheat the oven to 190°C (375°F, Gas Mark 5). Melt 25g/1oz of the butter in a small pan. Take one sheet of filo pastry and brush it with some of the melted butter. Top with a second sheet, brush with more butter and repeat with the remaining sheets. Brush the final layer with butter, then use a 13cm/5 inch round plain cutter to cut out 4 discs. Line four 10cm/4 inch tart tins with these discs and place them in the refrigerator to chill.

Heat 7g/¼oz of the remaining butter in a small pan and cook the shallots and garlic in it until soft. Remove from the heat and transfer to a bowl. Add the egg, crumbs and walnuts and stir together to form a smooth paste. Chill until firm, then stir in the cream and season to taste with salt and pepper.

Heat 50g/2oz of the butter in a frying pan, add the courgettes, season and cook until lightly golden. Remove from the pan and leave to cool.

Take the filo tarts out of the refrigerator and spread the walnut frangipane over the base of each. Arrange the courgette slices attractively on top.

Melt the remaining butter in a small pan and stir in the thyme leaves. Brush this thyme butter over the surface of each tart, then season with a little celery salt, if using, and black pepper. Bake in the preheated oven for about 10 minutes, until the pastry is crisp. Remove carefully from the tins and serve at once.

WINE NOTES

A South African Sauvignon

Kirsch-Emmenthal Fondue with Herb Polenta Boccancini

What could be nicer than a table of friends, good wine and a well-flavoured fondue! Boccancini literally means 'small mouthfuls'. You could also serve a selection of blanched seasonal vegetables for dipping into the fondue.

1 tbsp cornflour
2 tbsp kirsch
1 clove garlic, halved
125ml/4fl oz dry white wine
250g/9oz Emmenthal cheese, grated
50g/2oz Gruyère cheese, grated
a little freshly grated nutmeg
¼ tsp bicarbonate of soda

FOR THE HERB POLENTA
300ml/½ pint milk
1 clove garlic, crushed
2 tbsp finely chopped mixed marjoram, oregano and basil
salt and freshly ground black pepper
75g/3oz polenta
50g/2oz unsalted butter (optional)
freshly grated nutmeg

WINE NOTES

A good Piedmontese, such as Barolo

First make the polenta. Put the milk, garlic, herbs and seasoning in a saucepan and bring to the boil. Rain in the polenta, stirring constantly, and mix until smooth, then reduce the heat and cook very gently for 30–40 minutes, stirring all the time. The mixture should form a thick mass that leaves the sides of the pan clean.

Spread the polenta in a buttered dish to form a layer about 1cm/½ inch thick. Leave to cool, then cut it into 2.5cm/1 inch squares. It can be prepared up to this stage the night before.

To serve, fry the polenta squares in the butter or, better still, grill them over an open flame. Keep them warm while you make the fondue.

Blend the cornflour to a paste with the kirsch and set aside. Rub a fondue dish or flameproof casserole with the garlic and pour in the wine. Bring slowly to the boil and add a little pepper. Gradually add the cheese, stirring constantly until it has melted. When the mixture begins to boil, thicken it with the cornflour paste and stir until smooth. Season with salt, pepper and a little nutmeg. Finally, stir in the bicarbonate of soda, which helps to break down the fat in the cheese and also to aerate the mixture. Serve immediately, accompanied by the polenta squares, which you spear with fondue forks and dip into the pan. Ideally the fondue should be kept warm over a low heat as you eat it so it does not set.

N.V. Suggestion

Diced cooked meats may also be used for dipping.

Walnut-crusted Goat's Cheese with Fried Potatoes and Spring Onions

50g/2oz walnuts, finely ground
15g/½oz fine white breadcrumbs
1 tsp ground cumin
salt and freshly ground black pepper
4 crottin de Chavignol goat's cheeses or
other small, firm goat's cheeses, sliced
horizontally in half
2 tbsp walnut oil
400g/14oz new potatoes
1 clove garlic, peeled
4 tbsp extra virgin olive oil
2 shallots, finely chopped
1 tsp black peppercorns, coarsely cracked

FOR THE DRESSING
2 tbsp red wine vinegar
6 tbsp walnut oil

1 tbsp hot water
a pinch of sugar
1 tsp finely chopped chives
4 spring onions, thinly sliced on the
diagonal

Mix together the walnuts, breadcrumbs, cumin, and seasoning. Dip the goat's cheese in the walnut oil, season, then roll it in the breadcrumb mixture to coat. Place on a baking sheet or a grill pan and set aside.

Cook the potatoes in boiling salted water until tender. Drain and refresh under cold running water, then peel and cut into slices 5mm/¼ inch thick. Crush the garlic clove lightly with a knife, then rub it over a frying pan. Add the olive oil and heat gently. Add the shallots and sweat for 1–2 minutes, then add the potatoes, raise the heat and fry until pale golden. Season with salt and coarsely cracked peppercorns.

Put the goat's cheeses under a moderately hot grill (or in a moderately hot oven) for about 3–4 minutes, until softened and golden. Meanwhile, make the dressing by whisking together the vinegar, oil, water and sugar and then stirring in the chives and spring onions. Put the fried potatoes on serving plates, top with the goat's cheese, pour a little of the dressing around and serve immediately.

Semi-Carpaccio of Vegetables

4 large cauliflower florets
4 large broccoli florets
12 young carrots, scraped clean, tops
left attached
8 baby turnips, trimmed
75g/3oz fresh ceps (optional)
12 baby leeks, trimmed
25g/1oz thin French beans, trimmed
50g/2oz shelled fresh broad beans
350ml/12fl oz vegetable stock
(see page 148)
2 tbsp sunflower oil
2 tbsp extra virgin olive oil
juice of 1 lemon

15g/½oz basil
15g/½oz chervil
15g/½oz chives
sea salt and coarsely cracked black pepper

Using a sharp knife or a mandoline, cut the cauliflower and broccoli florets into slices about 3mm/⅛ inch thick, being as careful as possible as they break easily. Slice the carrots and turnips lengthways to the same thickness and then slice the ceps, if using. Leave the leeks, French beans and broad beans whole.

Heat the vegetable stock in a large pan and blanch the vegetables separately in it for about 20–30 seconds; they should still retain some crunch. Mix together the oils, lemon juice and 2–3 tablespoons of the stock to make a dressing. Place the warm vegetables in a shallow dish and pour over the dressing, then leave to cool.

To serve, arrange the vegetables on plates, then drizzle over the dressing, sprinkle over some cracked black pepper and coarse sea salt and garnish with the herbs.

Radicchio Paupiettes with Goat's Cheese on an Artichoke and Olive Casserole

1 head of radicchio
6 tbsp extra virgin olive oil
1 onion, finely chopped
1 tsp cumin seeds
4 crottin de Chavignol goat's cheeses or
other small firm goat's cheeses, cut in
half horizontally

FOR THE CASSEROLE
8 globe artichokes
3 tbsp extra virgin olive oil
1 onion, chopped
2 cloves garlic, crushed
125ml/4fl oz white wine
200ml/7fl oz Tomato Concassée (see
page 151)
100ml/3½fl oz vegetable stock (see
page 148)
1 tbsp oregano
75g/3oz green olives, stoned

WINE NOTES

An Alsace Pinot Noir

Preheat the oven to 180°C (350°F, Gas Mark 4). To make the casserole, prepare the artichokes as described on page 139 and cut each one into 8 wedges. Heat the oil in an ovenproof dish, add the onion and garlic and cook gently for 2 minutes before adding the artichoke wedges. Pour in the wine and bring to the boil, then add the tomato concassée and stock and cover with a lid. Transfer to the preheated oven and cook for 10–12 minutes, turning the artichokes often. Add the oregano and olives and then cook for a further 5 minutes.

Meanwhile, remove 8 large outer leaves from the radicchio, blanch them in boiling water for 1 minute, then refresh in iced water and dry in a cloth. Shred the remaining radicchio finely. Heat 4 tablespoons of the olive oil in a pan, add the shredded radicchio, onion and cumin and sweat gently until just tender, then leave to cool.

Lay out the blanched radicchio leaves, put half a goat's cheese in the centre of each one, then top with the radicchio, onion and cumin filling. Roll them up to secure the filling, then brush with the remaining olive oil. The paupiettes are best grilled over an open flame grill but you could bake them for 5 minutes in the oven at the same temperature as the artichoke casserole. Arrange the paupiettes on the artichoke casserole and serve immediately.

Aubergine Schnitzels with Red Onion Vinaigrette

This makes a good light lunch dish or, in smaller quantities, an appetizer. The schnitzels are filled with the classic combination of mozzarella, basil and tomato.

8 basil leaves
olive oil for cooking
2 medium aubergines, cut into rounds
1cm/½ inch thick (you need 16 slices altogether)
salt and freshly ground black pepper
½ tbsp Dijon mustard
1 buffalo mozzarella cheese, cut into 8 slices
6 plum tomatoes, peeled and cut into slices 1cm/½ inch thick
4 eggs
50g/2oz white breadcrumbs
75g/3oz Parmesan cheese, finely grated

FOR THE DRESSING
2 tbsp champagne vinegar
3 tbsp extra virgin olive oil
3 tbsp vegetable oil
1 red onion, finely diced or cut into thin rings
1 tbsp finely chopped chives

Blanch the basil leaves in a small pan of boiling water for a few seconds, then drain, refresh under cold water and dry.

Pour enough olive oil into a frying pan to coat the base thinly, then fry half the aubergine slices over a moderate heat until golden; remove and drain on paper towels. Fry the remaining aubergine and leave to cool.

Lay out 8 aubergine slices on a work surface and season them. Brush each one with a smear of Dijon mustard, lay a slice of mozzarella on top, then two slices of tomato, side by side, and season again. Now place one basil leaf on top, then finally another aubergine slice. Press the sandwiches together firmly, then chill them for about an hour.

In a bowl, beat together the eggs, breadcrumbs and Parmesan and season well. In a separate bowl, whisk together all the ingredients for the dressing and set aside.

Heat some olive oil in a large frying pan, dip each aubergine schnitzel into the egg mixture to coat and then fry them in the hot oil for about 3–4 minutes or until golden brown, turning them over half way through. Put the schnitzels on a serving dish, pour round the red onion vinaigrette and serve immediately.

N.V.
Suggestion

Add a slice of cooked ham to the vegetable layers.

Cushions of Crottin Cheese with Olive and Tomato Tapenades

These are good with a rocket salad dressed simply with olive oil. For a more substantial meal, serve them on a bed of Sweet and Sour Peperonata (see page 114).

2 sheets of filo pastry
50g/2oz clarified butter (see page 151)
4 crottin de Chavignol goat's cheeses or other small firm goat's cheeses, each cut horizontally into 3 pieces
2 tbsp Black Olive Tapenade (see page 153)

8 basil leaves
2 tbsp Tomato Tapenade (see page 153)

Preheat the oven to 190°C (375°F, Gas Mark 5). Lay one sheet of filo pastry out on a work surface, brush with clarified butter and top with the second sheet. Brush with more butter, then cut the pastry into quarters to give 4 squares. Place a piece of cheese in the centre of each one, top each with half a spoonful of black olive tapenade and place a basil leaf on top.

Now add a second piece of cheese, followed by half a spoonful of the tomato tapenade and finally, the last piece of cheese topped with another basil leaf, to form a three-tiered effect.

Brush the exposed pastry with clarified butter, then fold it securely over the filling. Cut off any excess pastry with a sharp knife or scissors. Brush the parcels with a little more butter and place on a baking sheet. Bake them in the preheated oven for about 8 minutes and then serve.

Macaroni Gratin with Piperade

You could add some fresh herbs, such as basil or chives, to the piperade.

150g/5oz macaroni
2 tbsp extra virgin olive oil
75g/3oz onion, chopped
½ red pepper, cut into strips
½ green pepper, cut into strips
1 clove garlic, crushed
4 tomatoes, peeled, deseeded and cut into strips
6 eggs, lightly beaten
salt and freshly ground black pepper
125ml/4fl oz double cream
25g/1oz Gruyère cheese, grated

Cook the macaroni in a large pan of boiling salted water until *al dente* (see pages 68–9), then drain through a colander, refresh in iced water, drain again and leave to dry.

To make the piperade, heat the olive oil in a pan and fry the onion until tender. Add the peppers and half the garlic and cook gently for 4–5 minutes, then stir in the tomatoes. Cook over a moderate heat for 8–10 minutes, until the liquid given off by the vegetables has almost evaporated. Add the eggs and some seasoning, then beat the eggs and vegetables lightly together with a fork until the eggs are just cooked. The mixture should be moist and fluffy.

Heat the cream in a pan with the remaining garlic and some salt and pepper. Stir in the pasta and heat through, then adjust the seasoning.

Divide the piperade between 4 serving dishes or bowls, top with the macaroni and sprinkle over the grated cheese. Bake in the oven at 200°C (400°F, Gas Mark 6) for 3–4 minutes or brown under a hot grill.

WINE NOTES

An Italian Cabernet Sauvignon or Merlot

Pasta,
Grains and Pulses

*This chapter takes a fresh look at the fabulous variety
of grains and pulses now available, such as barley,
black beans, matzoh meal and couscous. It also
includes everything you need to know about pasta,
from making your own dough, to preparing
simple noodle dishes and exotic stuffed pastas. Also,
here are some colourful risottos, and stuffings
for vegetables.*

*The recipes are inexpensive, easy to prepare and
satisfying and the majority of them can be the main
dish in a dinner party or a family meal. There are
some exotic dishes featuring flavours of the orient
alongside more summery ones using beetroot, rocket
and sweet tomato with garlic – quite delicious.*

Basic Pasta Dough

Fresh pasta is now available from Italian delicatessens but I find that it tends to be dry and sometimes only marginally better than packaged pasta. It is well worth taking the time to prepare fresh pasta at home. It is very simple to make and keeps for up to 3 days in the refrigerator or 1 month in the freezer; should you wish, make double the amount.
If you have a food processor the job is even easier but, call me a traditionalist, I still prefer to make the dough by hand.
Below are instructions for both methods.

250g/9oz strong plain flour
a pinch of salt
2 eggs plus 1 egg yolk, lightly beaten
1 tbsp extra virgin olive oil
1 tbsp water

BY HAND

Sift the flour and salt on to a clean work surface (marble is ideal), forming it into a mound, then make a well in the centre with your fingers. Pour the beaten eggs into the well, add the oil and water, then gradually mix the flour in towards the centre with your fingertips until all the ingredients have been combined into a paste.

Gather the dough into a neat ball and knead for 4–5 minutes or until it is smooth and elastic. Cover with cling film and leave to rest for up to 30 minutes.

BY FOOD PROCESSOR

Put the flour, salt and olive oil in a food processor and process for a few seconds to combine. Add the beaten eggs and process until the mixture forms a mass. This will only take a few seconds and it is important not to overwork the dough. Remove the dough from the food processor. If it is a little dry, knead in the water; if it is too wet, sprinkle with a little flour. Cover and leave to rest as above.

ROLLING OUT THE DOUGH

Rolling out pasta dough by hand can be tedious but with a small, hand-operated pasta machine it becomes a lot easier. These machines vary in size and price but a fairly basic model will do the job. However, you will need to buy a cutting attachment if you want to make noodles.

Cut the rested pasta dough into 4–6 pieces. Put the machine on setting no. 1, then feed a piece of dough through the rollers, which should be lightly floured to prevent the pasta sticking. Put the machine on setting no. 2 and pass the dough through again. Continue in this way until the dough is very thin – you may need to go to no. 4 or 5 setting. Cut the pasta to the desired shape (see below) and leave it to dry for 10 minutes.

CUTTING THE PASTA

For spaghetti, linguine, fettuccine and other narrow ribbon shapes simply attach the relevant noodle cutter to the pasta machine and feed the pasta through.

For lasagne and cannelloni, cut sheets of pasta into 10 × 7.5cm/4 × 3 inch rectangles. For pappardelle, cut the pasta into long ribbons 2.5cm/ 1 inch wide.

To make ravioli, brush a sheet of pasta with water and then place on it small teaspoonfuls of stuffing, about 5cm/2 inches apart, in rows. Cover with a second sheet of pasta, press down gently, then cut the pasta into squares with a pasta wheel or a sharp knife. Check the edges are well sealed. Ravioloni are made in the same way as ravioli but are slightly larger.

To make tortellini, cut the rolled-out pasta into circles with a 7.5cm/ 3 inch plain cutter. Place a good teaspoonful of filling on one half of each circle, then brush the edges with a little water and fold in half, pressing gently to seal the edges together. Carefully fold each semi-circle around your finger to form a crescent shape.

COOKING PASTA

It is important to cook pasta just before you serve it. Fill a very large saucepan with water (about 4 litres/ 7 pints water for 450g/1lb pasta), add a good pinch of salt and a little olive oil, then bring it to the boil. The oil helps prevent the pasta sticking, which is particularly useful when cooking large sheets of pasta such as lasagne.

Add the pasta to the boiling water and give it a quick stir, then put the lid on until the water returns to the boil. Remove the lid and cook for 1½–2½ minutes or until the pasta is *al dente* (literally, 'to the teeth') – this means that the pasta should retain a little bite to it, and the time taken will vary depending on the thickness of your pasta. Stuffed pasta, which should be cooked at a gentle simmer so it doesn't break apart, will take about 4–5 minutes. Dried pasta takes considerably longer to cook (about 8–10 minutes) but the method should be same.

Drain the pasta thoroughly in a large colander, then either return it to the pan and stir in a little butter or olive oil and seasoning, or proceed as directed in the recipe. Serve the pasta immediately on warmed plates or in shallow bowls.

VARIATIONS

BLACK OLIVE PASTA

Purée or very finely chop 50g/2oz rinsed black olives and then proceed as for Basic Pasta, adding the olives to the flour with the eggs. No salt is necessary as the olives are already salty.

GRAINY MUSTARD PASTA

Proceed as for Basic Pasta, adding 1 tablespoon of wholegrain mustard to the flour with the eggs.

KITCHEN TOBACCO PASTA

In the 16th century mushrooms were hung on string and left to dry in the kitchen, then ground to a powder to make soups, etc. They resembled tobacco in appearance, hence the name.

Replace 15g/½oz of the flour with 15g/½oz dried wild mushrooms that have been ground to a fine powder in a food processor or grinder. Add the powdered mushrooms to the flour and proceed as for Basic Pasta.

SPICED PASTA

I like to flavour pasta dough with exotic spices, such as cumin, coriander, curry powder, saffron or even sweet spices such as cinnamon. Add about ½ teaspoon ground spice to the flour and proceed as for Basic Pasta.

PESTO PASTA

200g/7oz basil, finely chopped
1 egg plus 1 egg yolk
1 tbsp extra virgin olive oil
½ tsp crushed garlic
1 tbsp freshly grated Parmesan cheese
salt and freshly ground black pepper
300g/11oz strong plain flour

Place the basil, eggs and oil in a blender or food processor and blitz until smooth. Make the dough as for Basic Pasta, adding the egg and basil mixture, garlic, Parmesan and seasoning to the flour.

SOY MILK PASTA

This is a useful recipe for people who cannot take cow's milk. It has a strong, earthy flavour.

300g/11oz strong plain flour
a pinch of salt
1 egg plus 3 egg yolks, beaten
6 tbsp soy milk
2 tbsp groundnut oil

Proceed as for Basic Pasta, adding the soy milk to the flour with the eggs.

Citrus Fettuccine with Mint and Courgettes al Cartoccio

Al cartoccio means 'in a paper bag' –
a surprisingly effective way of cooking
all sorts of food, even pasta. Fresh
fettuccine is best here, preferably home-
made, but dried pasta can be used
instead.

50g/2oz unsalted butter
2 large courgettes, cut in half
lengthways, seeds scooped out, sliced
5mm/¼ inch thick
zest and juice of 2 oranges
zest and juice of 1 lemon
100ml/3½fl oz crème fraîche or double
cream
8 mint leaves, finely chopped
salt and freshly ground black pepper
450g/1lb fresh fettuccine (see page 68)
freshly grated nutmeg

FOR THE VEGETABLE NOODLES
1 large carrot, peeled
1 large courgette, peeled
1 small leek, trimmed

WINE NOTES

An Italian Sauvignon
or Chardonnay

First, cut out 4 circles of baking parchment or aluminium foil at least 25cm/10 inches in diameter. Fold in half to make a centre crease, then unfold and lightly butter around the edges of each circle. Set aside. Preheat the oven to 230°C (450°F, Gas Mark 8).

Prepare the vegetable noodles by cutting the carrot and courgette into long slices 3mm/⅛ inch thick with a fine slicer or mandoline and then cutting them in half lengthways. Cut the leek finely by hand to the same size as the carrot and courgette strips. Blanch the vegetables in boiling salted water for 30 seconds, refresh them in iced water and then drain and dry them.

To make the sauce, heat half the butter in a small frying pan, add the sliced courgettes and sauté until just tender. Remove from the heat and set aside. Put the orange and lemon zest and juice in a separate pan and cook over a high heat until reduced in volume by a third. Pour in the cream, bring to the boil, then reduce the heat and cook until the sauce is thick enough to coat the back of a spoon. Cut the remaining butter into small pieces and whisk it into the sauce a little at a time; finally add the chopped mint. Season to taste and then stir in the courgettes. Keep the sauce warm while you cook the pasta.

Cook the fettuccine in a large pan of boiling salted water until *al dente* (see pages 68–9), then drain in a colander. Stir the pasta and the vegetable noodles into the cream sauce until well coated and season to taste with salt, pepper and nutmeg.

Divide the pasta between the paper or foil circles, placing it to one side of the centre crease. Fold over the other half of the paper and seal with tiny pleats. Place the pasta packages on a baking sheet and bake in the preheated oven for 4–5 minutes, until puffed and lightly browned. Immediately transfer the packages to serving plates and let your guests open them themselves.

A simpler serving idea is to place each portion of the cooked pasta mixture on an ovenproof serving plate or bowl, then wrap the entire plate in paper and place it in the oven.

N.V.
Suggestion

Serve with a fillet of veal or breast of chicken.

Stracci with Spring Vegetables and Bitter Leaves

Stracci *means rags or cloths, an apt description for these little sheets of pasta, which are arranged casually on the plate.*

1 quantity of Basic Pasta Dough (see
page 68)
1 bunch of watercress
1 bunch of rocket
450g/1lb fresh broad beans, shelled
1 tbsp mascarpone cheese
salt and freshly ground black pepper
200g/7oz fresh peas, shelled
12 green asparagus spears, cut into
4 pieces on the diagonal
freshly grated nutmeg

FOR THE HERB BUTTER SAUCE
125ml/4fl oz White Butter Sauce (see
page 150), kept warm
1 tbsp chopped basil
1 tbsp chopped tarragon
1 tbsp chopped chives
½ tbsp lemon juice

Roll out the pasta as described on page 68 and cut it into twenty 10× 6cm/4×2½ inch rectangles. Mix together the watercress and rocket; set both aside.

Cook 150g/5oz of broad beans in boiling salted water until very tender; drain well and purée in a liquidizer with the mascarpone. Season and keep warm.

For the sauce, return the white butter sauce to the pan and stir in the herbs and lemon juice. Cook the remaining broad beans, the peas and asparagus in separate pans of boiling water until just tender, drain, refresh in iced water, drain again and stir into the sauce.

Cook the pasta in plenty of boiling salted water until *al dente* (see pages 68–9), drain well and season.

To serve, make a small mound of bean purée on 4 warmed plates and top with the pasta sheets. Place a bouquet of the mixed watercress and rocket on top of each one. Pour the sauce around the pasta and serve immediately.

Oven-glazed Spaghetti with Walnut Sauce

150g/5oz walnut halves
2 cloves garlic, crushed
175ml/6fl oz double cream
25g/1oz fresh white breadcrumbs
100g/4oz Parmesan or Pecorino cheese,
finely grated
freshly grated nutmeg
salt and freshly ground black pepper
450g/1lb dried spaghetti
1 egg yolk

Preheat the oven to 200°C (400°F, Gas Mark 6). Process 75g/3oz of the walnuts until finely ground.

Put the garlic and cream in a saucepan and bring to the boil, then reduce the heat and simmer until the cream is reduced by half its original volume. Stir in the breadcrumbs and 75g/3oz of the grated cheese, then add the ground walnuts and season with nutmeg, salt and pepper.

Cook the spaghetti in plenty of boiling salted water until *al dente* (see pages 68–9), then drain, retaining 3–4 tablespoons of the cooking water in the pan. Pour the walnut sauce into the pan, add the egg yolk and whisk well. Put the drained spaghetti back to the pan and stir until bound together.

Adjust the seasoning to taste, then transfer the mixture to an ovenproof dish, sprinkle with the remaining cheese and put in the preheated oven for 5–8 minutes to glaze. Sprinkle with the remaining walnuts and serve.

N. V.
Suggestion

Add some diced cooked ham or prosciutto to the spaghetti mixture before baking.

Soy Milk Pasta with Thai Vegetable Curry

You can experiment with an endless variety of vegetables for this dish. The Thai sauce also doubles up as an excellent spicy soup.

½ quantity of Soy Milk Pasta (see page 69)
8 large cauliflower florets
8 large broccoli florets
100g/4oz sweet potato or pumpkin, cut into 1cm/½ inch dice
1 tbsp sesame oil
2 tbsp vegetable oil
¼ tsp crushed garlic
1 tsp grated fresh ginger root
1 carrot, thinly sliced
25g/1oz mangetout, finely shredded
25g/1oz beansprouts
25g/1oz daikon radish (mooli), finely shredded
25g/1oz shiitake mushrooms
4 spring onions, finely shredded
2 tbsp melted unsalted butter
coriander leaves, to garnish

FOR THE THAI SAUCE
2 tbsp vegetable oil
1 onion, roughly chopped
½ small red pepper, coarsely chopped
1 red chilli, deseeded and chopped
1 clove garlic, crushed
1 tsp finely chopped fresh ginger root
½ tsp turmeric
1 tsp ground coriander
½ tsp curry powder
150ml/¼ pint chicken or vegetable stock (see pages 148, 149)

100ml/3½fl oz coconut milk
1 lemon grass stalk, roughly chopped
4 tbsp double cream
1 heaped tsp arrowroot (optional)
2 level tbsp chopped coriander leaves
juice of ½ lime
salt and freshly ground black pepper

First make the sauce. Heat the oil in a pan, add the onion and red pepper and cook gently for 2 minutes before adding the chilli, garlic, ginger and spices. Cook over a low heat for a further 5–8 minutes, until the spices are cooked out and become sandy in texture. Add the stock, coconut milk and lemon grass and cook for about 12–15 minutes, until the sauce thickens and reduces in volume. Pour in the cream and cook for a further 2 minutes. If the sauce is too thin, blend the arrowroot with a little water to form a paste, stir it into the sauce and cook for 1–2 minutes.

Strain the sauce and then stir in the coriander leaves, lime juice and seasoning to taste. The sauce can be made well in advance and will keep for 2–3 days in the refrigerator.

Roll out the pasta dough and cut it into eight 10 × 7.5cm/4 × 3 inch sheets (you will need to make the whole quantity of pasta but the rest can be frozen for later use).

Blanch the cauliflower, broccoli and sweet potato or pumpkin in a large pan of boiling salted water for 2 minutes.

Drain them, plunge them into iced water to refresh, drain again and dry on a cloth.

Heat the sesame oil and vegetable oil in a frying pan, add the garlic and ginger and leave to infuse for 2 minutes over a low heat. Add the blanched vegetables and fry over a moderate heat for 1–2 minutes. Then add the remaining vegetables and stir-fry for 1–2 minutes only, so that they retain their crispness. Season to taste.

Cook the pasta in a large pan of boiling salted water (see pages 68–9), then drain well. Season and brush with the melted butter.

Place a sheet of pasta on each serving plate, arrange the vegetables on top, then cover with another sheet of pasta. Fold back the pasta to expose the vegetables; pour the sauce around, garnish with coriander leaves and serve immediately.

WINE NOTES

An Alsace Riesling or Gewürztraminer

*Citrus Fettucine with Mint and Courgettes al Cartoccio (page 70),
and Soy Milk Pasta with Thai Vegetable Curry*

Soy-glazed Linguine with Ginger and Tofu

450g/1lb fresh or dried linguine
25g/1oz unsalted butter
2 tbsp sesame oil
1 clove garlic, crushed
25g/1oz fresh ginger root, peeled and finely shredded
1 carrot, finely shredded
2 spring onions, finely shredded
75g/3oz shiitake or Chinese black mushrooms, shredded
2 heads of bok choy, roughly shredded
1 yellow pepper, finely shredded
2 tbsp dry sherry
4 tbsp ketjap manis (sweet Indonesian soy sauce)
1 tbsp rice wine vinegar
90ml/3fl oz vegetable stock (see page 148)
100g/4oz firm tofu, cut into 8mm/⅜ inch cubes
2 tbsp coriander leaves
2 red chillies, deseeded and cut into very thin rings

Cook the linguine in plenty of boiling salted water until *al dente* (see pages 68–9), then drain well and keep it warm.

Heat the butter, sesame oil, garlic and ginger in a frying pan for about 1 minute over a moderate heat. Add the carrot, spring onions, mushrooms, bok choy and yellow pepper and sauté for 1 minute. Stir in the sherry, ketjap manis and rice vinegar, bring to the boil and cook for a further 2 minutes.

Add the vegetable stock and cook until it is reduced to a light, syrupy consistency. Add the drained linguine and stir until the sauce forms a glaze around the pasta. Finally, stir in the tofu, then transfer the mixture to a serving dish, sprinkle with the coriander and chilli and serve at once.

N.V.
Suggestion

Add some langoustine or diced salmon to the vegetables.

Olive Pappardelle with Oven-dried Tomatoes and Walnut and Basil Oil

2 × quantity of Black Olive Pasta, made into pappardelle (see pages 68–9)
4 tbsp extra virgin olive oil
75g/3oz Oven-dried Tomatoes (see page 153), thinly sliced
freshly grated nutmeg

FOR THE WALNUT AND BASIL OIL
50g/2oz walnuts
10 large basil leaves
2 cloves garlic, chopped
150ml/¼ pint extra virgin olive oil
1 tsp lemon juice
a pinch of sugar
freshly grated nutmeg
salt and freshly ground black pepper

Put all the ingredients for the walnut and basil oil in a blender or food processor and blend to a coarse pulp. Adjust the seasoning with sugar, nutmeg, salt and pepper if necessary.

Cook the pappardelle in plenty of boiling salted water until *al dente* (see pages 68–9), then drain. Heat the oil in a pan, add the tomato strips and pasta and mix together. Season with salt, pepper and nutmeg.

Transfer to warmed serving bowls and coat with the walnut and basil oil. Serve immediately.

Plum Tomato Tortellini with Courgettes in a Garlic-infused Broth

You need a lot of tomatoes for this recipe so the best time to prepare it is during the summer when they are plentiful, well-flavoured and cheap. I like to try different fillings in the tortellini – usually ones with a Mediterranean bias such as ratatouille and ricotta or aubergine and goat's cheese.

3 tbsp extra virgin olive oil
1.5kg/3½lb firm, ripe plum tomatoes, skinned, halved and deseeded
1 clove garlic, crushed
½ tsp sugar
6 basil leaves, roughly chopped
salt and freshly ground black pepper
1 quantity of Basic Pasta Dough (see page 68)
2 courgettes, finely shredded
freshly grated nutmeg

FOR THE GARLIC BROTH
4 large cloves garlic, peeled and halved
300ml/½ pint chicken or vegetable stock (see pages 148, 149)
50g/2oz unsalted butter, cut into small pieces

First prepare the tomato filling for the tortellini: heat the oil in a pan, add the tomato halves and cook gently for 1 minute, until softened. Add the garlic and sugar and continue to cook over a low heat for about 10 minutes, until the tomatoes become slightly caramelized. Transfer to a bowl and leave to cool. Drain the tomatoes of excess juice if necessary, then chop them roughly and stir in the basil. Add salt and pepper to taste.

Roll out the pasta and make the tortellini as described on page 68, filling them with the tomato mixture; they can be kept in the refrigerator until required.

To make the garlic broth, put the garlic cloves and stock into a pan, bring to the boil, then lower the heat and simmer gently for 30 minutes or until the stock has reduced by half its original volume. Strain the stock to remove the garlic, then whisk the butter into the stock a piece at a time to make a light, buttery broth. Adjust the seasoning, then stir in the shredded courgettes.

Cook the tortellini in a large pan of gently simmering water (see pages 68–9) until *al dente*, then drain and season with nutmeg, salt and pepper. Divide the pasta between warmed serving bowls, coat with the garlic broth and serve immediately.

Vegetable Orzo Kedgeree

This vegetarian version of kedgeree uses orzo, a rice-shaped pasta, instead of rice. You can, of course, make it with basmati rice if you prefer. Although kedgeree is traditionally served as a breakfast dish this one makes a satisfying lunch.

*1 large aubergine, cut into
1cm/½ inch dice
salt and freshly ground black pepper
50g/2oz unsalted butter
2 shallots or 1 onion, finely chopped
1 carrot, finely diced
1 red pepper, very finely diced
1 cauliflower, cut into
walnut-sized florets
50g/2oz fresh or frozen peas
1 tbsp finely chopped coriander leaves
½ tsp finely chopped fresh ginger root
2 cardamon pods, crushed
¼ tsp cinnamon
2 tsp Home-made Curry Powder (see
page 154)
a good pinch of saffron
225g/8oz orzo (rice-shaped pasta)
1 litre/1¾ pints vegetable stock (see
page 148)*

Put the diced aubergine in a colander, salt it lightly and leave for 30 minutes. Rinse under cold running water and pat dry.

Heat the butter in a heavy saucepan, add the shallots or onion and cook gently until tender. Add the aubergine and all the remaining vegetables, together with the coriander leaves and spices, and cook over a low heat for 2 minutes. Stir in the orzo, then pour on the stock and bring to the boil. Reduce the heat and season lightly, then cover with a tight-fitting lid and cook very gently for about 15–20 minutes, checking occasionally and stirring. The pasta should be *al dente* and the kedgeree should still be moist. Serve immediately.

N.V.
Suggestion

In classic kedgeree tradition, add some steamed fish such as salmon or haddock just before serving.

WINE NOTES

A dry and fresh white Rhône

Pasta-enveloped Terrine with Mediterranean Flavours

This terrine looks spectacular but is not at all difficult to prepare. It can also be made with some soft goat's cheese or mozzarella added to the vegetable layers.

6 aubergines, cut lengthways into slices
1cm/½ inch thick
salt and freshly ground black pepper
1 quantity of Pesto Pasta (see page 69)
6 red peppers
2 cloves garlic, thinly sliced
a small bunch of thyme
125ml/4fl oz extra virgin olive oil
freshly grated nutmeg

FOR THE BASIL BUTTER
20 large basil leaves, passed through a
juice extractor (see page 146)
75g/3oz unsalted butter, melted

FOR THE DRESSING
6 tbsp extra virgin olive oil
2 tbsp champagne vinegar
10 basil leaves, shredded
3 tomatoes, peeled, deseeded and diced
(optional)

SERVES 10–12

Put the aubergine slices in a colander and salt them lightly, then leave for up to 1 hour. Rinse thoroughly under cold running water, drain and leave to dry.

Roll out the pasta dough and cut it into ten 15 × 10cm/6 × 4 inch rectangles. Cook them in plenty of boiling water until *al dente* (see pages 68–69) then remove them from the pan and immerse in iced water to refresh them. Leave them on a cloth or kitchen paper to dry.

Preheat the oven to 200°C (400°F, Gas Mark 6). Cut the red peppers in half through the stem, remove the seeds and fill the cavities with the garlic and thyme. Put them in a dish and brush with 4 tablespoons of the olive oil, then cover with aluminium foil and bake in the preheated oven for 20–25 minutes or until tender. Meanwhile, fry the aubergine slices in the remaining oil until golden and tender. When the peppers are done, remove the thyme and garlic and peel the peppers while they are warm.

To make the basil butter, stir the basil juice into the melted butter and season lightly. Brush the cooked pasta sheets on one side with the butter and season with nutmeg, salt and pepper.

To assemble the terrine, line a terrine or 900g/2lb loaf tin with cling film, making sure that you have a good overlap at each side, then line it with the pasta sheets, buttered side inside, overlapping them neatly so there are no gaps and allowing the ends of the pasta to overhang the terrine all round. Arrange the cooked aubergine and pepper slices in the terrine in alternate layers with the pasta. Brush each layer with basil butter and press down gently so the mixture is compact. When the terrine is full, fold over the overhanging pasta and cling film, then put a small board and a heavy weight on top and refrigerate for 12–24 hours.

Just before you serve the terrine, mix together all the ingredients for the dressing and season to taste. Carefully turn out the terrine and peel off the cling film. Cut it into slices with a very sharp serrated knife and arrange on serving plates. Pour a little of the dressing round and serve.

WINE NOTES

An Australian Semillon Chardonnay

Swiss Chard and Date Ravioloni with Roasted Peppers

1 quantity of Basic Pasta Dough or
Spiced Pasta made with saffron
(see page 68)
50g/2oz butter
1 yellow pepper, roasted, peeled and cut
into thin strips
1 red pepper, roasted, peeled and cut
into thin strips
4 sage leaves, chopped
25g/1oz walnuts, chopped

FOR THE FILLING
25g/1oz butter
1 small clove garlic, crushed
zest and juice of ½ lemon
150g/5oz Swiss chard, cooked and
finely chopped
1 tbsp balsamic vinegar
100g/4oz ricotta cheese
50g/2oz fresh dates, stoned and
finely chopped
25g/1oz Parmesan cheese, grated
salt and freshly ground black pepper
freshly grated nutmeg

To make the filling, heat the butter in a pan with the garlic and lemon zest. Add the Swiss chard and cook gently for 2–3 minutes. Add the balsamic vinegar and cook for 1 minute more. Transfer to a bowl and leave to cool, then add the ricotta, dates, Parmesan and lemon juice. Season with salt, pepper and nutmeg.

Roll out the pasta dough and make the ravioloni as described on page 68, filling each one with a good tablespoon of the Swiss chard mixture and making each of them about 6cm/2½ inches square.

Cook the ravioloni in a large pan of boiling salted water until *al dente* (see pages 68–9), then remove them from the pan, using a slotted spoon, and drain well.

To finish, heat the butter in a pan until it is foaming, add the roasted pepper strips, chopped sage and walnuts and season lightly. Arrange the ravioloni on serving plates and coat with the foaming butter and roasted peppers. Serve immediately.

WINE NOTES

A Rioja, preferably a Reserva red

*S*wiss Chard and Date Ravioloni with Roasted Peppers, and
Cannelloni of Ratatouille with Ricotta and Basil (page 80)

Cannelloni of Ratatouille with Ricotta and Basil

The ricotta may be replaced by another cheese, such as goat's cheese or grated Gruyère.

4 tbsp extra virgin olive oil
75g/3oz unsalted butter
1 small onion, finely diced
1 clove garlic, crushed
1 courgette, cut into 8mm/⅜ inch dice
1 aubergine, cut into 8mm/⅜ inch dice
1 red pepper, cut into 8mm/⅜ inch dice
1 green pepper, cut into
8mm/⅜ inch dice
salt and freshly ground black pepper
4 tbsp double cream
100g/4oz ricotta cheese
8 sheets of fresh lasagne (see page 68)
4 tbsp vegetable stock or water
12 basil leaves, cut into fine strips, plus
extra to garnish
shavings of fresh Parmesan cheese, to
garnish

Preheat the oven to 200°C (400°F, Gas Mark 6). Heat half the olive oil with 15g/½oz of the butter in a heavy-based saucepan, then add the onion and garlic and cook gently for 1 minute. Add the diced courgette, aubergine and peppers and cook over a moderate heat for about 5 minutes or until all the vegetables are tender. Season to taste, then remove from the heat and leave to cool.

Put the cream in a small pan and boil until it is reduced by half. Add the ricotta cheese and mix well, then stir in the cooled ratatouille.

Cook the lasagne in a large pan of boiling salted water until *al dente* (see pages 68–9); drain well, lay the lasagne on a clean tea-towel and pat dry. Brush with a little of the remaining olive oil and season with salt and pepper. Put some of the ricotta cheese and ratatouille mixture in the centre of each piece of lasagne and roll up, overlapping the ends, to make cannelloni. Place the cannelloni in a well-buttered ovenproof dish; add the vegetable stock or water and the remaining olive oil. Cover with buttered foil and place in the oven for about 10 minutes or until heated through.

To serve, remove the cannelloni from the oven and arrange 2 on each serving plate. Pour the juices from the cannelloni dish into a small saucepan and heat gently. Cut the remaining butter into small pieces and whisk it into the pan a little at a time until it emulsifies and forms a creamy sauce. Season to taste, then pass through a fine sieve. Add the basil leaves to the butter sauce and pour it over the cannelloni. Garnish with shavings of Parmesan cheese and basil leaves and serve them immediately.

WINE NOTES

A good Italian red, such as Barolo or Brunello

Mushroom Rigatoni with Spinach Soufflé

In this recipe pasta is baked under a light, thin soufflé crust. It is very good served with a little White Butter Sauce (see page 150) with fresh herbs. For a real treat, use a selection of wild mushrooms instead of button mushrooms.

400g/14oz dried rigatoni
100g/4oz unsalted butter
4 shallots, finely chopped
225g/8oz button mushrooms, finely chopped
salt and freshly ground black pepper
125ml/4fl oz double cream

FOR THE SOUFFLÉ
50g/2oz unsalted butter
50g/2oz plain flour
200ml/7fl oz milk, heated with an onion cloute (see page 149)
400g/14oz fresh spinach, cooked, well drained and finely chopped
freshly grated nutmeg
3 egg yolks
4 egg whites

Preheat the oven to 200°C (400°F, Gas Mark 6). Cook the pasta in plenty of boiling salted water until *al dente* (see pages 68–9), then drain. Heat the butter in a pan, add the shallots and mushrooms and cook until tender. Stir in the drained pasta and season lightly, then add the cream and cook gently for 2 minutes, until the pasta is bound in the sauce. Keep the pasta warm.

To make the spinach soufflé, melt the butter in a heavy-based saucepan, stir in the flour to form a roux and cook for 1–2 minutes over a gentle heat. Gradually stir in the milk and cook gently for 5–8 minutes, stirring occasionally. Add the cooked and chopped spinach and season to taste with salt, pepper and nutmeg, then remove from the heat and beat in the egg yolks.

In a large bowl, beat the egg whites with a pinch of salt until they form stiff peaks. Stir about a quarter of them into the spinach mixture and then gently fold in the rest.

Put the mushroom and pasta mixture into a well-buttered 25cm/ 10 inch gratin dish. Carefully pour over the soufflé mixture and bake in the preheated oven for 20–25 minutes, until well risen and brown. Serve immediately.

Beetroot and Ricotta Ravioli with Rocket Pesto

450g/1lb raw young beetroot
2 tbsp finely chopped spring onions
or chives
150g/5oz ricotta cheese
50g/2oz Parmesan cheese, grated, plus
extra to serve
freshly grated nutmeg
salt and freshly ground black pepper
1 quantity of Basic Pasta Dough (see
page 68)
1 quantity of Rocket Pesto (see
page 152)

Cook the beetroot in a large pan of boiling water until tender, then drain, refresh in cold water and drain again. Peel the beetroot and cut them into 1cm/½ inch dice, then dry on kitchen paper. Place in a bowl and mix carefully with the spring onions or chives and the ricotta and Parmesan so that the beetroot is incorporated but doesn't 'bleed' too much into the cheese. Season with nutmeg, salt and pepper to taste.

Roll out the pasta and make the ravioli as described on page 68, filling them with the beetroot and cheese mixture. Cook them in plenty of simmering salted water until *al dente* (see pages 68–9) and then drain well.

Heat the rocket pesto gently in a large pan (if it is too thick, add a little cooking water from the ravioli), then stir in the ravioli and season to taste. Arrange on warmed serving plates and serve sprinkled with Parmesan.

Penne with Broccoli, Raisins and Chick Peas

During a brief period working in an Indian restaurant, I was astonished to encounter chick peas cooked in tea. It was explained to me that this aids the digestion and gives the chick peas a nice colour but at the same time does nothing to harm their flavour.

50g/2oz chick peas, soaked overnight
and then drained
tea for cooking the chick peas (optional)
150g/5oz broccoli, divided into
small florets
450g/1lb dried penne
4 tbsp extra virgin olive oil
1 clove garlic, crushed
25g/1oz raisins, soaked in warm water
until plump

25g/1oz black olives, chopped
175ml/6fl oz Grilled Tomato Sauce (see
page 152)
12 basil leaves, chopped
2 tbsp sun-dried tomatoes, cut into
5mm/¼ inch dice
freshly grated nutmeg
salt and freshly ground black pepper
25g/1oz unsalted butter
2 tbsp pine kernels, toasted
2 tbsp fresh Parmesan shavings
(optional)

Put the chick peas in a pan, cover with fresh water or with tea and bring to the boil. Reduce the heat and simmer for 1–2 hours, until tender. Drain and set aside.

In separate pans, cook the broccoli florets and the penne in boiling salted water until *al dente*, then drain and keep warm.

Heat the olive oil in a large heavy frying pan, add the garlic and cook over a gentle heat until it is tender but not browned. Stir in the raisins, olives, chick peas, tomato sauce, basil and sun-dried tomatoes, then add the drained pasta and toss well. Heat through, then season with nutmeg, salt and pepper. Meanwhile, melt the butter in a small pan and toss the broccoli florets in it to heat through. Serve the pasta topped with the broccoli and pine kernels, and with a sprinkling of Parmesan shavings, if using.

Fragrant Tomato Rice with Rosewater, Cinnamon and Vermicelli

An elegant rice pilaff with Middle Eastern flavours. You can use it as a stuffing for vine leaves or other leaves such as Swiss chard or spinach.

100g/4oz vermicelli
75g/3oz unsalted butter
1 onion, finely chopped
200g/7oz basmati or long grain rice
2 tsp tomato purée
a pinch of sugar
450ml/¾ pint vegetable stock (see page 148)
salt and freshly ground black pepper
cinnamon, to taste
rosewater, to taste

3 tbsp flaked almonds, toasted
50g/2oz raisins, soaked in warm water until plump

Preheat the oven to 200°C (400°F, Gas Mark 6). Crush the vermicelli in your hands into pieces about 2.5cm/1 inch long. Heat the butter in a heavy-based casserole, add the vermicelli and cook for about 1 minute or until golden. Add the onion and rice and stir to coat them with the butter. Then add the tomato purée and a good pinch of sugar and stir again.

Pour in the vegetable stock, stir well, then bring to the boil and season lightly. Cover with a lid and place in the preheated oven for about 20 minutes or until the rice is cooked.

Remove from the oven and stir in cinnamon and rosewater to taste. The rice should be quite well scented. Scatter the toasted almonds and raisins over the top and serve.

N.V.
Suggestion

Add some sautéed chicken livers to the rice.

Green Risotto with Fresh Herb Juice

I occasionally garnish this risotto with a small selection of vegetables, such as courgettes, artichokes, broccoli, etc.

600ml/1 pint vegetable stock (see page 148)
100g/4oz unsalted butter
2 shallots, finely chopped
1 clove garlic, crushed
250g/9oz Arborio rice
90ml/3fl oz white wine
125g/4½ oz mixed herbs, such as chervil, parsley and basil, passed through a juice extractor (see page 146)
salt and freshly ground black pepper

Bring the stock to the boil in a saucepan and keep it at a gentle simmer while you make the risotto. Melt 40g/1½oz of the butter in a heavy-based pan, add the shallots and garlic and cook gently for a few minutes until tender. Add the rice and mix well to coat the rice with the butter and give it a nice sheen.

Pour in the wine and cook until it is reduced to half its original volume. Over a moderate heat, add a ladleful of the stock and stir until it is absorbed. Keep adding the stock a ladleful at a time, stirring constantly, until the rice is tender but still retains a little bite. Towards the end of the cooking, add the stock in smaller quantities and check whether the rice is done. It should take about 25 minutes in all, and the consistency of the finished risotto should be fairly loose without being sloppy. If you use up all the stock before the rice is sufficiently cooked, add boiling water half a ladleful at a time, as necessary.

When the rice is cooked, mix in the herb juice. Stir in the remaining butter, season to taste with salt and pepper and serve immediately.

Oriental Black Risotto with Basmati Rice

This risotto uses mushroom stock and soy sauce, which give it a dark, inky appearance. It is one of my favourite rice dishes and I first made it on the television programme 'Hot Chefs'.

50g/2oz unsalted butter
1 small onion or shallot, finely chopped
½ tsp finely chopped garlic
½ tsp finely chopped fresh ginger root
250g/9oz basmati rice
2 tsp Chinese five-spice powder
750ml/1¼ pints Brown Mushroom Stock
(see page 149)
salt and freshly ground black pepper
2–3 tbsp dark soy sauce

FOR THE VEGETABLE GARNISH
4 tbsp sesame oil
50g/2oz unsalted butter
14 small shiitake mushrooms, halved
½ tsp finely chopped garlic
½ tsp finely chopped fresh ginger root
25g/1oz beansprouts
1 small carrot, finely shredded
12 mangetout, finely shredded
¼ red pepper, finely shredded
¼ green pepper, finely shredded
15g/½oz daikon radish (mooli), finely shredded
2 spring onions, finely shredded
16 coriander leaves (optional)

Heat the butter in a large, heavy-based saucepan, add the onion or shallot, garlic and ginger and cook for 1 minute without browning. Add the rice and stir well, then stir in the five-spice powder. Pour in the stock and bring to the boil, stirring occasionally. Add a little salt and pepper, reduce the heat and simmer, uncovered, for 15–20 minutes, stirring frequently with a wooden spoon, until the rice is *al dente* and nearly all the stock has evaporated. If there is still a lot of liquid left when the rice is done, raise the heat to boil it away. The rice should still be quite moist.

While the risotto is cooking, prepare the vegetable garnish. Heat 1 tablespoon of the sesame oil and 15g/½oz of the butter in a wok or large frying pan and sauté the mushrooms until tender, then remove them from the pan, set aside and keep warm. Heat the remaining oil and butter in the same pan over a moderate heat, then add the garlic and ginger and leave to infuse for a few minutes. Add all the vegetables and sauté until cooked but still crisp. Season with salt and pepper.

To serve, add soy sauce to taste to the risotto, then divide it between serving plates or bowls. Top with the vegetable garnish, the reserved mushrooms and the coriander leaves, if using, and serve at once.

N.V.
Suggestion

Arrange the risotto and garnish on the plates as described above, then top with some fried or grilled squid or grilled chicken.

WINE NOTES

A Shiraz from South Australia

Risotto Variations: Beetroot and Barolo Risotto (page 87), Green Risotto with Fresh Herb Juice (page 83), White Asparagus and Pea Risotto with Mascarpone, Lemon and Parsley (page 86), Oriental Black Risotto with Basmati Rice

White Asparagus and Pea Risotto with Mascarpone, Lemon and Parsley

White asparagus is highly prized in Europe. It has a very short season so keep a look out for it. Our own English springtime asparagus may be used in its place, of course.

16 firm white asparagus spears
600ml/1 pint vegetable stock (see page 148)
100g/4oz unsalted butter
2 shallots, finely chopped
250g/9oz Arborio rice
90ml/3fl oz champagne or dry white wine
1 tbsp freshly grated Parmesan cheese
2 tbsp mascarpone cheese
salt and freshly ground black pepper
100g/4oz peas, cooked
zest of 1 lemon
1 tbsp chopped flat-leaf parsley

Peel the asparagus spears, reserving the peelings, and cut the asparagus into thin slices on the diagonal. Poach it in lightly salted boiling water to cover. When it is just tender, remove from the pan with a slotted spoon, refresh in iced water and drain well, then set aside. Add the asparagus peelings to the water and simmer for a further 10 minutes to obtain a stronger asparagus stock. Strain through a fine sieve; you should have about 100–125ml/3½–4fl oz of stock. Put this in a pan with the vegetable stock, bring to the boil, then keep it at a simmer while you make the risotto.

Melt half the butter in a heavy-based saucepan, add the shallots and cook gently for a few minutes until they are tender. Add the rice and stir well to coat it with the butter. Over a moderate heat, add the champagne or dry white wine and a little of the stock and stir until the liquid is absorbed. Keep adding the stock a ladleful at a time, stirring constantly, until the rice is tender but still retains a little bite. Towards the end of the cooking, add the stock in smaller quantities and check whether the rice is done. It should take about 25 minutes in all, and the consistency of the finished risotto should be fairly loose without being sloppy. If you use up all the stock before the rice is sufficiently cooked, add boiling water half a ladleful at a time, as necessary.

When the rice is cooked, fork in the Parmesan and the mascarpone and season to taste. Melt the remaining butter in a saucepan, briefly toss the asparagus and the peas in it to heat through, and season. Stir the vegetables into the risotto, then divide between 4 serving plates and sprinkle with the lemon zest and parsley. Serve immediately.

WINE NOTES

A light Australian Semillon, preferably from New South Wales

Beetroot and Barolo Risotto

Unlike most risottos, this one is made with a red wine base. It also includes beetroot juice, which not only adds flavour but makes a visually stunning dish. Some grilled tender young leeks or courgettes go well with it.

600ml/1 pint vegetable stock (see page 148)
100ml/3½fl oz Barolo, or Valipolicella or other full-bodied red wine
juice of 1 raw beetroot (see page 146)
1 bay leaf
1 sprig of thyme
100g/4oz unsalted butter
2 shallots, finely chopped
1 small clove garlic, crushed
250g/9oz Arborio rice
2 tbsp good-quality red wine vinegar, such as Cabernet Sauvignon
salt and freshly ground black pepper

Place the stock, wine, half the raw beetroot juice and the bay leaf and thyme in a pan and bring to the boil. Reduce the heat and simmer gently for 10 minutes.

Meanwhile, melt half the butter in a heavy-based saucepan and gently cook the shallots and garlic in it for a few minutes until tender. Add the rice and stir to coat well with the butter. Over a moderate heat, add a ladleful of the wine-infused stock and stir until it is absorbed. Keep adding the simmering stock a ladleful at a time, stirring constantly, until the rice is tender but still retains a little bite. Towards the end of the cooking, add the liquid in smaller quantities and check whether the rice is done. It should take about 25 minutes in all, and the consistency of the finished risotto should be fairly loose without being sloppy. If you use up all the stock before the rice is sufficiently cooked, add boiling water half a ladleful at a time, as necessary.

Finally, stir in the remaining beetroot juice, then add the remaining butter and the vinegar and season to taste. Serve immediately.

WINE NOTES

A Chianti or fairly spicy red with herbal overtones

N.V.
Suggestion

Top with a piece of grilled turbot or sea bass drizzled with a little olive oil and scattered with fresh herbs.

Toasted Almond Matzoh with Roasted Garlic, Parmesan and Wild Mushrooms

4 cloves garlic
75g/3oz flaked almonds
6 tbsp extra virgin olive oil
4 shallots, finely chopped
175g/6oz matzoh meal
1 litre/1¾ pints milk, boiled
100g/4oz salted butter
salt and freshly ground black pepper
freshly grated nutmeg
4 tbsp clarified butter (see page 151)
4 tbsp fresh Parmesan shavings
150g/5oz fresh wild mushrooms, such as girolles, oyster, ceps, cut into pieces
1 tbsp chopped parsley
2 tbsp chopped sage
1 tbsp lemon juice

WINE NOTES

A Beaune, or light red Burgundy from the Côte de Beaune area

Preheat the oven to 180°C (350°F, Gas Mark 4). Wrap 3 of the garlic cloves in aluminium foil and bake in the oven for 25–30 minutes until very tender and mushy. Carefully peel off the skin and pass the garlic through a fine sieve to make a purée. Toast the flaked almonds by mixing them with a little of the olive oil, spreading them out on a baking sheet and placing them in the preheated oven until golden. Leave to cool, then blitz them in a food processor until roughly ground. Set aside.

To make the matzoh, heat a third of the oil in a pan, add the shallots and cook gently for 5 minutes until soft. Add the roasted garlic, then rain in the matzoh meal, running it through your fingers in a slow steady stream. Pour on the boiled milk and beat until thoroughly combined. Cook gently for 5–8 minutes, stirring from time to time, then fold in the almonds and 25g/1oz of the butter and stir until all is well bound together. Season with salt, pepper and nutmeg to taste. Using a spatula, scrape the mixture on to a shallow buttered baking sheet or dish, dip the spatula in water and spread out the dough to form an even square, about 1cm/½ inch thick. Place in the refrigerator to set for up to 4 hours (this may be made a day in advance).

Dip a knife or cutter into flour and cut out 8 squares or rectangles from the matzoh dough. Brush them with the clarified butter then place them on a baking sheet and place under a hot grill or bake in the oven at 200°C (400°F, Gas Mark 6) until golden. Arrange the Parmesan shavings on top of the matzoh squares, then return them to the hot oven or under the hot grill until golden and bubbly. Transfer them to a serving dish.

Heat the remaining oil in a pan, add the mushrooms and sauté gently for a few minutes. Meanwhile, thinly slice the remaining garlic clove. Add the sliced garlic and the herbs to the mushrooms and season to taste. Scatter the mushroom mixture over the matzoh squares.

Put the remaining butter in the pan and cook over a high heat until it browns and gives off a nutty fragrance. Add the lemon juice and coat the mushrooms and matzoh with this mixture. Serve immediately.

Note: I also like to serve this dish with a piquant vinegar butter sauce instead of with the lemon butter.

In a small saucepan, cook 1 chopped shallot with 4 tablespoons of balsamic vinegar and 150ml/¼ pint of vegetable stock until a syrupy consistency is achieved. Then whisk in 75g/3oz of butter, cut in small pieces, to form a sauce. Adjust the seasoning and serve with the fried wild mushrooms and toasted almond matzohs.

Spicy Fruit Tabbouleh

325g/12oz cracked wheat (bulgar),
soaked in plenty of cold water for 45
minutes and then drained
½ cucumber, peeled, deseeded and
chopped
4 spring onions, chopped
2 tbsp chopped mint
1 orange, peeled and cut into segments
(see page 47)
3 tomatoes, peeled, deseeded and chopped
1 red pepper, chopped
1 tbsp chopped basil
100g/4oz fresh pineapple, chopped
1 papaya, peeled, deseeded and chopped
100g/4oz melon, chopped

FOR THE DRESSING
1 red chilli, deseeded and finely chopped
300ml/½ pint water
juice of 3 limes
2 tbsp honey
¼ tsp finely chopped fresh ginger root
125ml/4fl oz extra virgin olive oil

SERVES 6–8

Put all the dressing ingredients except the oil in a pan and bring to the boil. Reduce the heat and simmer for 3–4 minutes, then remove from the heat and leave to cool.

Squeeze out any excess water from the cracked wheat and dry the grains in a clean cloth. Place it in a large bowl and add all the remaining salad ingredients. Mix well together.

Whisk the olive oil into the cooled dressing, then taste. The flavour should be quite tart, so add a little more lime juice if necessary. Mix the dressing with the salad and serve.

Stuffed Onions with Pinto Falafel

4 large onions, about 225g/8oz
each, peeled
250g/9oz pinto beans, cooked
2 tbsp tahini
1 clove garlic, crushed
½ tsp ground cumin
15g/½oz plain flour
½ tsp baking powder
1 tbsp chopped parsley
2 tbsp chopped coriander
1 tbsp chopped mint
salt and freshly ground black pepper
cayenne pepper
a little melted butter, for brushing
4 slices of soft fresh goat's cheese
(optional)

Preheat the oven to 200°C (400°F, Gas Mark 6). Blanch the onions in a large pan of boiling water for 3–4 minutes, then remove and leave to cool.

Purée the cooked pinto beans in a food processor, then transfer to a bowl and add the tahini, garlic and cumin. Mix in the flour, baking powder and herbs and season to taste with salt, pepper and cayenne.

Slice a third off the top of each onion and carefully remove the inner flesh, leaving 2 or 3 layers of onion to form a sturdy wall.

Chop the onion flesh and the slices removed from the top and add to the pinto falafel mixture. Fill the onions with this mixture, then place them in a lightly oiled ovenproof dish, brush them with a little butter and bake in the preheated oven for 45 minutes, until golden.

Top each onion with the goat's cheese, if using, and bake for a further 10 minutes. Serve with a good tomato sauce or a crisp salad.

WINE NOTES

*A red Côte du Rhône
or Gigondas*

Mediterranean Cassoulet with Mixed Pulses and Harissa

Harissa is a hot spicy paste used in Middle Eastern cookery, made from red chillies, caraway and coriander.

4 tbsp extra virgin olive oil
1 onion, chopped
2 cloves garlic, crushed
1 large red pepper, cut into 2cm/ ¾ inch dice
1 large yellow pepper, cut into 2cm/ ¾ inch dice
1 aubergine, cut into 2cm/¾ inch dice
2 courgettes, cut into 2cm/¾ inch dice
1 tbsp tomato purée
4 tomatoes, peeled, deseeded and roughly chopped
½ tbsp brown sugar
½ tsp harissa paste, or to taste
125ml/4fl oz dry white wine
900ml/1½ pints Dark Vegetable Stock (see page 148)
100g/4oz haricot beans, soaked overnight and then drained
100g/4oz brown lentils, soaked overnight and then drained
1 tbsp chopped rosemary
1 bay leaf
¼ tsp fennel seeds

FOR THE MILLET CRUST
100g/4oz millet
75g/3oz fresh white breadcrumbs
90g/3½oz softened unsalted butter
3 tbsp black olives, finely chopped
salt and freshly ground black pepper

Preheat the oven to 160°C (325°F, Gas Mark 3). Heat the olive oil in a pan, add the onion and garlic and cook for 1–2 minutes, until golden. Add the peppers, aubergine and courgettes and cook for 8–10 minutes, until golden. Stir in the tomato purée, tomatoes, sugar and harissa and cook for a further 5 minutes.

Add the wine, stock, haricot beans, lentils, herbs and fennel seeds and bring to the boil. Transfer to an ovenproof dish, cover with a lid and cook in the preheated oven for 1 hour, or until the pulses are tender.

Meanwhile, cook the millet in a large pan of boiling salted water for about 20 minutes or until tender, then drain. Mix it with all the other ingredients for the crust and season lightly. Remove the cassoulet from the oven and top with the crust, then return to the oven for a further 20 minutes until the crust is golden brown.

WINE NOTES

A Hungarian Chardonnay or a spicy Alsace white

N.V. Suggestion

Add duck confit and Toulouse sausage to the cassoulet.

*Mediterranean Cassoulet with Mixed Pulses and Harissa,
and Spicy Fruit Tabbouleh (page 89)*

Vegetarian Couscous with Saffron and Hara Masala

This is my light version of couscous: the couscous and the vegetables are blended at the last moment and the sauce is served separately. In this way the vegetables keep their colour and freshness. Hara masala is a blend of fresh herbs and spices used in Indian cooking.

FOR THE COUSCOUS
250ml/8fl oz hot chicken or vegetable stock (see pages 148, 149)
a pinch of saffron
50g/2oz unsalted butter
2 shallots or 1 onion, finely chopped
200g/7oz couscous
salt and freshly ground black pepper
2 tbsp extra virgin olive oil

FOR THE HARA MASALA
2 tbsp finely chopped coriander leaves
1 tbsp finely chopped mint
1 fresh green chilli, finely chopped

FOR THE VEGETABLES
2 tbsp extra virgin olive oil
2 small red onions, cut into wedges
2 cloves garlic, thinly sliced
1 tbsp hara masala, or to taste (see opposite)
½ tsp ground cumin
¼ tsp cinnamon
4 yellow courgettes, thinly sliced
2 carrots, thinly sliced
75g/3oz pumpkin, cut into 1cm/ ½ inch cubes
1 red pepper, cut into 1cm/½ inch dice
1 large sweet potato, cut into 1cm/ ½ inch cubes
900ml/1½ pints vegetable stock (see page 148)
50g/2oz raisins, soaked in warm water until plump
2 tbsp flaked almonds
12 cherry tomatoes
75g/3oz chick peas, cooked
300ml/½ pint Spicy Tomato Sauce (see page 152)

To prepare the couscous, heat the stock in a pan, add the saffron and simmer for 5 minutes. Heat the butter in a separate pan, add the shallots or onion and cook gently for 3–4 minutes, until softened. Stir in the couscous, cover, remove from the heat and leave to stand for 5–6 minutes or until the couscous has swollen and can be fluffed up with a fork. Cover again and leave for 5 minutes longer. Season to taste, stir in the oil and keep warm.

For the hara masala, simply mix everything together. To make the vegetable stew, heat the oil in a pan, add the onions and garlic and sauté until browned. Add the spices and cook for 3–4 minutes until they give off their fragrance. Add all the vegetables except the tomatoes, cover with the vegetable stock and cook over a gentle heat until the vegetables are tender and the liquid has evaporated. Add the raisins, almonds and cherry tomatoes and heat through. Stir in the couscous pilaff and chick peas. Heat gently, season to taste and serve, accompanied by the remaining hara masala, if you like. Pass the tomato sauce at the table separately.

WINE NOTES

An organic Sauvignon Blanc

N.V.
Suggestion

Serve with grilled or roast lamb cutlets or loin.

Barley-filled Dolmas with Lentil Sauce

150g/5oz pearl barley
12 green cabbage leaves
zest and juice of ½ lemon
1 tsp chopped parsley
2 tbsp pine kernels, lightly toasted
2 tbsp raisins or currants, soaked in
warm water for a few minutes
until plump
½ tsp allspice
½ tsp chopped oregano
a little oil or melted butter, for brushing
150ml/¼ pint yogurt
100g/4oz feta cheese, crumbled
2 egg yolks

FOR THE LENTIL SAUCE
100g/4oz Puy lentils, soaked overnight
and then drained
2 tbsp vegetable oil
½ onion, finely chopped
1 clove garlic, crushed
½ tsp dried or fresh mixed herbs, such as
thyme and rosemary
1 tbsp tomato purée
125ml/4fl oz Tomato Concassée (see
page 151)
salt and freshly ground black pepper

To make the lentil sauce, place the soaked lentils in a saucepan, cover with cold water and bring to the boil. Skim off any impurities from the surface, then reduce the heat and simmer gently for 20–25 minutes or until tender. Drain the lentils and reserve the cooking liquid. You should have about 150ml/¼ pint; top it up with water if necessary.

Heat the oil in a pan, add the onion and garlic and cook gently until tender. Add the herbs and lentils, then stir in the tomato purée and concassée. Finally stir in the reserved cooking liquid, bring to the boil and simmer until the sauce is fairly thick and chunky. Season to taste and keep to one side (this sauce may be made a day in advance and reheated when required).

Preheat the oven to 200°C (400°F, Gas Mark 6). To make the dolmas, cook the pearl barley in a pan of boiling water for about 30–40 minutes or until tender. Meanwhile, blanch the cabbage leaves in a large pan of boiling salted water for about 5–8 minutes, until wilted; refresh them in cold water, drain and dry well. When the barley is cooked, drain thoroughly and transfer it to a bowl; while it is still hot, add the lemon zest and juice, parsley, pine kernels, raisins or currants, allspice and oregano, and season to taste.

Lay out the blanched cabbage leaves on a work surface and cut away the hard central core of each one. Place a good tablespoon of the barley mixture in the centre of each leaf, then fold up the bottom and sides of each leaf to enclose the filling and roll them up securely.

Pour the lentil sauce into a shallow ovenproof dish. Brush the dolmas with a little oil or butter and place them on top of the sauce. Mix together the yogurt, feta cheese and egg yolks and pour this over the dolmas. Bake in the preheated oven for about 10 minutes, until browned, then serve.

WINE NOTES

A Zinfandel

*Barley-filled Dolmas with Lentil Sauce (page 93) and
Roasted Vegetables on Black Bean Chilli*

Roasted Vegetables on Black Bean Chilli

I first discovered the pleasures of chillies and black beans through my close colleague and friend, Dean Fearing, chef at the Lanesborough's sister hotel in Dallas, Texas, who specializes in Southwest cuisine. I like to serve this dish with some soured cream or crème fraîche and freshly grated Cheddar cheese.

Don't be put off by the suggested inclusion of chocolate in the chilli. Mexicans love to use dark bitter chocolate in their native dishes, especially with spices and chillies, and the result is surprisingly good.

6 tbsp extra virgin olive oil
1 onion, finely chopped
2 cloves garlic, crushed
1 green chilli, finely chopped
1 tsp chilli powder
½ tbsp ground cumin
½ tbsp chopped oregano
1 litre/1¾ pints chicken or vegetable stock (see pages 148, 149)
250g/9oz black turtle beans, soaked overnight and then drained
3 tomatoes, peeled and diced
1 green pepper, finely diced
50g/2oz plain chocolate, melted (optional)
salt and freshly ground black pepper
675–900g/1½–2lb assorted vegetables suitable for roasting, such as parsnips, courgettes, aubergines, mushrooms, potatoes, baby carrots, etc., peeled if necessary and trimmed, or cut into bite-sized chunks

Heat 2 tablespoons of the oil in a heavy-based saucepan. Add the onion, garlic, green chilli, chilli powder, cumin and oregano and sweat gently until tender. Add the stock, bring to the boil and stir in the black turtle beans. Add the chopped tomatoes and green pepper, then reduce the heat and simmer gently, stirring occasionally, for 1–1½ hours or until the beans are tender. As the beans cook they will form their own sauce. When they are tender, stir in the melted chocolate, if using, and season if necessary.

While the beans are cooking, preheat the oven to 200°C (400°F, Gas Mark 6). Put the vegetables for roasting in a bowl and toss them in the remaining olive oil to coat; season lightly. Place them on a baking sheet and roast until golden; root vegetables will take about 30 minutes and courgettes, mushrooms, aubergines, etc. about 15 minutes. Serve the chilli topped with the roasted vegetables.

WINE NOTES

A dry Californian Riesling

Main Courses
and Accompaniments

One of the most difficult decisions when planning a vegetarian menu is what to do for the main course. But what constitutes a main course? People's ideas vary. One thing for sure is that it should be something fairly substantial. My own personal way around this problem is to replace the meat element of the meal with protein such as eggs, pulses, cheese. I find by doing this the only thing left to do is to decide on accompanying vegetables if you so wish.

This chapter includes some of my favourite vegetable dishes, any of which makes a perfect centrepiece for a vegetarian meal, plus some delicious vegetable accompaniments. These include some unusual roasted vegetable purées.

Potato and Goat's Cheese Brûlée with Chanterelles

This is a savoury version of crème brûlée, with the sugar topping replaced by crisp baked potato slices. Only small portions are needed as it is very rich; serve with a green salad.

1 large baking potato, such as Cyprus, peeled
4 tbsp clarified butter (see page 151)
salt and freshly ground black pepper
450g/1lb floury potatoes, peeled
150g/5oz soft goat's cheese
200ml/7fl oz double cream
100ml/3½fl oz milk
2 eggs
2 egg yolks
freshly grated nutmeg

FOR THE GARNISH
50g/2oz unsalted butter
2 shallots, finely chopped
½ small clove garlic, thinly sliced
75g/3oz small chanterelle or button mushrooms, thickly sliced
1 tbsp chopped parsley

Preheat the oven to 200°C (400°F, Gas Mark 6). Using a vegetable slicer or mandoline, cut the baking potato into 12 wafer-thin slices. Dip them into the clarified butter, season lightly, then place on a baking sheet and bake in the preheated oven for 4–5 minutes, until golden and crisp. (These potato sheets may be prepared earlier in the day.) Remove from the oven and reduce the temperature to 130°C (250°C, Gas Mark ½).

Put the floury potatoes in a pan of cold salted water and bring to the boil. Cook until tender, then drain and pass through a fine sieve or a food mill. Mash the goat's cheese with a fork and beat it into the potatoes while they are still hot.

Bring the double cream and milk to the boil in a saucepan, add the potato and goat's cheese mixture and stir well together, then remove from the heat. Beat in the eggs and egg yolks and season with salt, pepper and nutmeg.

Take 4 small soufflé moulds or other individual ovenproof dishes, about 250ml/8fl oz in capacity, and brush them lightly with a little clarified butter. Pour in the potato and goat's cheese mixture, then place the moulds in a shallow ovenproof dish or roasting tin and pour in enough boiling water to come a third of the way up the sides. Place in the oven and cook for 30–40 minutes or until the mixture is just setting and is springy to the touch.

Remove from the oven and keep it warm while you prepare the garnish.

For the garnish, heat the butter in a small pan, add the shallots and garlic and sweat together for 1 minute. Raise the heat to high and add the mushrooms. Sauté until the mushrooms are tender, then stir in the parsley. Season to taste.

To serve, top each potato and goat's cheese brûlée with a little of the mushroom mixture and then with the crisp potato slices. Serve immediately.

WINE NOTES

A white Côte du Rhône or white Châteauneuf du Pape

*P*otato and Goat's Cheese Brûlée
with Chanterelles

Leek Polenta Roll with Melted Cherry Tomatoes

I find that the traditional slow-cooking polenta works best here.

750ml/1¼ pints vegetable stock (see page 148)
450g/1lb baby leeks, trimmed
salt and freshly ground black pepper
freshly grated nutmeg
1 clove garlic, crushed
175g/6oz polenta
100g/4oz sweetcorn kernels, preferably fresh but canned sweetcorn will do
4 tbsp Genoese Pesto Sauce (see page 152)
1–3 tbsp clarified butter (see page 151)
a little butter, for frying

FOR THE MELTED CHERRY TOMATOES
250g/9oz cherry tomatoes
4 tbsp extra virgin olive oil
1 clove garlic, crushed
2 tbsp finely chopped basil
1 tsp sherry vinegar
1 tbsp lemon juice

Bring the vegetable stock to the boil in a large, heavy-based pan and then reduce the heat. Add half the leeks and cook for 3–4 minutes or until tender. Remove the leeks with a slotted spoon, drain well and leave to cool. Season with salt, pepper and nutmeg and set aside.

Add the garlic to the vegetable stock and bring it back to the boil. Lower the heat, then slowly sprinkle in the polenta, stirring all the time. Continue to stir with a wooden spoon until the mixture thickens and leaves the sides of the pan clean – this will take up to 40 minutes. If it becomes too thick to work, add a little more stock or water.

When the polenta is ready, stir in the sweetcorn kernels, then add the pesto, beat well together and adjust the seasoning to taste.

To assemble the leek polenta roll, brush a little clarified butter over a large piece of aluminium foil, about 30cm/12 inches long. With a palette knife, carefully spread a 1cm/½ inch layer of polenta over an area 20cm/8 inches square. Carefully arrange the cooked leeks on top in rows from one side to the other, pressing them down into the polenta as you do so. Season lightly and roll the polenta and leeks up with the foil like a Swiss roll. Tighten both ends of the foil like a bonbon and put the roll in the refrigerator for about 2 hours, until firm.

Blanch the remaining baby leeks in boiling water for 3 minutes, then drain, refresh them in iced water and dry. Fry them gently in a little butter just to heat through and then season to taste.

Preheat the oven to 150°C (300°F, Gas Mark 2). Combine all the ingredients for the melted cherry tomatoes in a baking dish and set aside. Remove the leek polenta roll from the refrigerator, remove the foil and, using a sharp knife, cut the roll into 2cm/¾ inch slices. Fry the slices in clarified butter or grill them until lightly golden and crispy. Meanwhile, bake the cherry tomatoes for 5 minutes until they are just beginning to soften. Season to taste. Serve the leek polenta roll garnished with the baby leeks and melted cherry tomatoes.

WINE NOTES

A Pinot Noir from New Zealand

*Q*uark and Courgette Boudins with Tarragon Sauce and Rocket (page 102),
and Leek Polenta Roll with Melted Cherry Tomatoes

Quark and Courgette Boudins with Tarragon Sauce and Rocket

Boudins are a French speciality sausage, white or black. This is my cheesy vegetarian alternative.

450g/1lb quark or cream cheese
50g/2oz plain flour
3 eggs
salt and freshly ground black pepper
freshly grated nutmeg
2 large courgettes
1 tbsp extra virgin olive oil
50g/2oz rocket leaves, stalks removed
125ml/4fl oz Tomato Concassée (see page 151)

FOR THE SAUCE
150ml/¼ pint White Butter Sauce, kept warm (see page 150)
1 tbsp finely chopped tarragon

Mix the cheese, flour and eggs together in a bowl and season with salt, pepper and nutmeg. Chill for up to 2 hours.

Thinly slice the courgettes, discarding the end slices; you should have 16 slices in all. Blanch them briefly in a large pan of boiling water then drain them well, refresh under cold running water and pat dry. Lightly butter eight 15cm/6 inch square pieces of aluminium foil and lay 4 overlapping courgette slices on each one. Place 2 good tablespoons of the cheese mixture in the centre of each square then carefully fold the short ends of the courgette slices over the cheese mixture and roll up to form a cylinder. Holding both ends of the foil, twist them to form a sort of bonbon, completely enclosing the filling.

Bring a large pan of water to the boil, reduce the heat to a simmer and add the boudins. Poach for 3–5 minutes, then remove from the pan with a slotted spoon.

For the sauce, return the white butter sauce to the pan, add the chopped tarragon and season to taste.

Heat the oil in a separate pan and cook the rocket leaves gently until wilted. Heat the tomato concassée and pour it into a serving dish or on to individual plates. Remove the foil from the boudins and place them on top of the tomato concassée. Pour the sauce around the boudins, top with the wilted rocket and serve immediately.

Blanquette of Young Vegetables in a Pea and Watercress Sauce

275g/10oz fresh peas, shelled
1.75 litres/3 pints vegetable stock (see page 148)
32 tender green asparagus spears, peeled
175g/6oz mangetout
175g/6oz broad beans, shelled
175g/6oz baby spring onions, trimmed
24 baby carrots, trimmed
24 baby turnips, trimmed
24 baby leeks, trimmed
4 tbsp crème fraîche

2oz/50g unsalted butter
24 watercress leaves, finely shredded

Cook the peas in boiling water until just tender, then remove about a third of them and refresh in iced water. Set aside. Continue cooking the remaining peas until they are very tender, then drain them and blend to a fine purée. Set aside.

Bring the vegetable stock to the boil in a pan, then cook all the remaining vegetables separately in it until just tender, removing them with a slotted spoon before adding the next lot. Put 500ml/18fl oz of the stock in a separate pan and stir in the crème fraîche. Bring to the boil and stir in the pea purée, butter and watercress.

Reheat the vegetables in the pea and watercress sauce, then ladle the mixture into 4 shallow bowls and serve .

Minestra

This simple, satisfying Italian vegetable stew is served topped with poached eggs and is not to be confused with the famous minestrone soup. It is traditionally accompanied by small pieces of stale bread such as ciabatta, for dunking.

6 tbsp extra virgin olive oil
1 clove garlic, crushed
1 tbsp chopped rosemary
½ tsp fennel seeds
100g/4oz cannellini beans, soaked overnight and then drained
1 litre/1¾ pints vegetable stock (see page 148) or water
100g/4oz Savoy or winter cabbage, roughly shredded
1 head of chicory, roughly shredded
1 fennel bulb, shredded
2 celery sticks, shredded
1 turnip, roughly shredded
12 cherry tomatoes
2 tbsp vinegar
4 eggs
salt and freshly ground black pepper
50g/2oz Pecorino cheese, coarsely grated

Heat 4 tablespoons of the oil in a large pan, then add the garlic, rosemary and fennel seeds and sweat gently for 2 minutes. Place the soaked cannellini beans on top and cover with the vegetable stock or water. Bring to the boil, then reduce the heat and simmer gently for 1 hour or until the beans are tender. You may need to add a little water while they are cooking. Drain them well, reserving the liquid, then strain the liquid and set it aside.

Heat the remaining oil in the same pan, add the cabbage and chicory and sweat gently, covered, for 3–5 minutes. Add the fennel, celery and turnip and sweat for a further 5 minutes. Pour in the strained cooking liquid, add the cooked beans and the cherry tomatoes and cook gently for 15 minutes, until all the vegetables are tender.

Meanwhile, bring a large pan of water to the boil and add the vinegar. Gently break the eggs into the water and poach for 3–4 minutes. Remove with a slotted spoon and drain well.

Just before serving, season the stew to taste and stir in the Pecorino cheese. Pour it into bowls, drizzle a little olive oil over each portion and top with a poached egg.

The eggs can be prepared in advance: when they are cooked, refresh them in iced water to halt the cooking, then reheat for 1 minute in boiling water before adding them to the stew.

N.V. Suggestion

Add 450g/1lb diced pancetta to the stew with the cabbage and chicory.

Creole Ratatouille

Creole Ratatouille

*A dish from the French
Caribbean Islands.*

*1 pumpkin, weighing about 1.25kg/3lb
a little clarified butter (see page 151)
or olive oil
salt and freshly ground black pepper
2 tbsp extra virgin olive oil
1 onion, sliced
4 cloves garlic, crushed
1 aubergine, cut into large dice, salted
for 30 minutes, then rinsed and drained
1 small red pepper, very thinly sliced
½ small green pepper, very thinly sliced
250g/9oz plum tomatoes, peeled,
deseeded and diced
100ml/3½ fl oz tomato juice
1 tbsp tomato purée
½ tbsp sugar
1 bay leaf
1 tsp dried herbes de Provence
100g/4oz courgettes, very thinly sliced
100g/4oz okra, trimmed (optional)
¼ cucumber, peeled, deseeded and very
thinly sliced
3 tbsp chopped basil
2 drops of Tabasco sauce*

Preheat the oven to 150°C (300°F, Gas Mark 2). Slice about 5cm/ 2 inches off the top of the pumpkin and scoop out the seeds. With a small sharp knife, make 6–8 small slashes in the pumpkin; this prevents it splitting during cooking. Brush the inside of the pumpkin with clarified butter or oil and season. Wrap it in foil and bake in the preheated oven for 1–1¼ hours, until tender but not mushy.

Meanwhile, heat the olive oil in a heavy-based saucepan, add the onion and garlic and cook until tender. Stir in the aubergine and peppers and cook over a gentle heat for 10–12 minutes, until they start to soften. Then add the diced tomatoes, tomato juice, tomato purée, sugar, bay leaf and herbs and cook until the tomatoes have softened. Finally add the courgettes, okra, cucumber and basil. Cook for a further 10–12 minutes until the vegetables are tender but still retain their colour.

Remove the vegetables from the pan with a slotted spoon and boil the liquid in the pan over a high heat until it becomes syrupy. Return the vegetables to the saucepan and add the Tabasco and salt and pepper to taste.

Fill the pumpkin with the ratatouille and return it to the oven for 10 minutes. Serve the ratatouille from the pumpkin, scooping out the pumpkin flesh with the vegetables. An alternative but more time-consuming method is to scoop out the pumpkin flesh raw, dice it and cook it with the ratatouille.

WINE NOTES

*A crisp, fragrant and spicy
Alsace Sylvaner or Riesling*

Potato Brandade Dumplings with Warm Niçoise Vinaigrette

When baby red peppers are in season I like to roast and peel them, then cut them in half and pipe in the potato dumpling mixture; bake and serve as below.

675g/1½lb baking potatoes
275ml/9fl oz milk or water
75g/3oz unsalted butter
4 cloves garlic, crushed
100g/4oz plain flour
4 eggs
freshly grated nutmeg
salt and freshly ground black pepper
1 tbsp freshly grated Parmesan cheese
sprigs of basil, to garnish

FOR THE VINAIGRETTE
4 tbsp extra virgin olive oil
½ onion, finely diced
1 courgette, finely diced
2 plum tomatoes, peeled, deseeded and finely diced
1 tbsp black olives, stoned and finely diced
½ tbsp lemon juice
90ml/3fl oz vegetable stock (see page 148)

Preheat the oven to 200°C (400°F, Gas Mark 6). Scrub the potatoes, dry them well, then prick them all over with a fork and bake for 1–1½ hours, until soft when pierced with a knife. Cut them in half, scoop out the flesh and pass it through a sieve. Leave the oven on but reduce the temperature to 180°C (350°F, Gas Mark 4).

Put the milk or water, butter and garlic in a saucepan and bring to the boil, then rain in the flour a little at a time, stirring constantly with a wooden spoon, until it forms a mass that will leave the sides of the pan clean.

Add the sieved potatoes to the pan and beat until thoroughly combined. Beat in the eggs one at a time, then season to taste with nutmeg, salt and pepper and leave to cool.

Generously butter a large shallow baking dish. Use 2 large tablespoons to mould the mixture into 12 quenelles: take a tablespoonful of the mixture, then shape it with the second spoon, turning it between the two. Arrange the quenelles in the dish, leaving a gap between each one to allow for expansion. Sprinkle them with the Parmesan and bake in the preheated oven for 10–12 minutes, until souffléed and golden.

Meanwhile make the vinaigrette. Heat 2 teaspoons of the oil in a pan, add the onion and cook for a few minutes, until tender. Add the courgette, tomatoes and olives and cook for 1 minute. Add the lemon juice and vegetable stock and bring to the boil, then remove from the heat, whisk in the remaining oil and season to taste.

Remove the potato dumplings from the oven, transfer to a serving dish, and pour the warm vinaigrette around. Serve immediately, garnished with sprigs of basil.

WINE NOTES

A white Côte de Duras, Chardonnay or Mâcon-Villages

Cep and Artichoke Crumble with Fresh Herbs

675g/1½ lb fresh ceps, or a mixture of
ceps and chestnut mushrooms
4 tbsp extra virgin olive oil
8 cooked artichoke hearts, cut into slices
5mm–1cm/¼–½ inch thick
50g/2oz unsalted butter
2 large shallots, finely chopped
2 cloves garlic, crushed
2 tbsp chopped black olives
salt and freshly ground black pepper

FOR THE HERB CRUST
175g/6oz fresh white breadcrumbs
150g/5oz unsalted butter, melted
2 tbsp finely chopped chervil
2 tbsp finely chopped flat-leaf parsley

Preheat the oven to 200°C (400°F, Gas Mark 6). Clean the mushrooms by wiping them with a damp cloth, then remove the stalks, cut them into 3mm/⅛ inch dice and set aside. Cut the mushroom caps into slices 5mm–1cm/¼–½ inch thick.

Heat the olive oil in a large frying pan and quickly fry the mushrooms and artichokes until golden. Remove from the pan and keep warm. Melt the butter in the pan, then add the shallots, garlic, diced mushroom stalks and olives. Cook gently until softened and then season to taste and remove from the heat.

Butter a 25cm/10 inch gratin dish and season the base lightly. Arrange the artichokes and ceps and the mushroom stalk mixture in alternate layers in the dish. Mix together all the ingredients for the herb crust, adding seasoning to taste. Sprinkle this mixture over the vegetables and bake in the preheated oven for about 10 minutes or until golden. Serve immediately. White Butter Sauce (see page 150) goes well with it.

WINE NOTES

A good cru Beaujolais, such as a Brouilly

Spinach, Pepper and Haloumi Rollatinis

3 tbsp extra virgin olive oil
4 spring onions, chopped
1 red pepper, finely chopped
600g/1lb 6oz spinach, washed and well
drained
2 eggs, beaten
100g/4oz Haloumi cheese, crumbled
2 tbsp chopped dill
freshly grated nutmeg
salt and freshly ground black pepper
12 sheets of 10×10/4×4 inch spring roll
pastry, or use filo pastry, cut to size
1 egg beaten with 1 tbsp water, to glaze

Preheat the oven to 180°C (350°F, Gas Mark 6). Heat the oil in a pan, add the spring onions and red peppers and sweat for 4–5 minutes until tender. Add the spinach and cook until it has wilted and all the excess moisture has evaporated. Leave to cool, then transfer to a bowl, stir in the eggs, cheese, dill and nutmeg and season to taste.

Lay out the pastry on a work surface and brush with a little beaten eggwash. Arrange some of the spinach filling at the bottom of each square. Fold the two sides into the middle, brush with eggwash again, then roll up.

Place the rollatinis on a greased baking sheet, brush with more eggwash and bake in the preheated oven for 10–12 minutes, until golden. Serve with a sauce, such as Grilled Tomato Sauce (see page 151).

Two-Onion Tart with Ceps

*T*wo-Onion Tart with Ceps

Tiny onion tarts can be made in the same way to serve as canapés, in which case you can omit the button onions and the cep garnish. If you can't get fresh ceps, substitute 25g/1oz dried ones and soak them in boiling water for up to 1 hour before using. Reserve the soaking water to add to the sauce.

1 quantity of Basic Shortcrust Pastry
(see page 155)
6 firm white Spanish onions, peeled
4 tbsp vegetable oil
1 tsp cumin seeds
450g/1lb small, firm button
onions, peeled
125ml/4fl oz Dark Vegetable Stock (see
page 148)
50g/2oz caster sugar
50g/2oz unsalted butter
salt

FOR THE GARNISH
75g/3oz unsalted butter
100g/4oz fresh ceps, thinly sliced
90ml/3fl oz Brown Mushroom Stock or
Dark Vegetable Stock (see page 148)
3 tbsp port
1 tbsp chopped parsley

Preheat the oven to 190°C (375°F, Gas Mark 5). Roll out the pastry and use to line a deep 20–23cm/8–9 inch plain flan tin. Line with grease-proof paper, fill with cooking beans and bake blind for 8–10 minutes. Remove the paper and beans and return to the oven for a further 5 minutes, then leave to cool.

Slice the Spanish onions in half through the root, remove the root and shred the onions very finely; this may be done with the shredder attachment of a food processor. Heat the vegetable oil in a heavy-based pan, add the sliced onions and cook gently for 10–15 minutes, until golden. Towards the end of the cooking time, add the cumin seeds and mix well together. Meanwhile, place the button onions in a small pan with the stock, sugar, butter, and salt to taste. Bring to the boil and cook over a high heat for 15–20 minutes, until the onions are cooked and caramelized.

Remove the pastry case from the flan tin and half fill it with the shredded onions, then arrange the glazed button onions on top so that they are level with the top of the pastry, packing them in very tightly with no gaps.

For the garnish, melt 25g/1oz of the butter in a small pan, add the mushrooms and cook for 2 minutes. Add the stock and the port and bring to the boil. Remove from the heat and whisk in the remaining butter a piece at a time until emulsified.

To serve, reheat the tart in the oven for 5 minutes. Cut it into 4 wedges and transfer them to serving plates; surround with the mushrooms and sprinkle with the chopped parsley.

WINE NOTES

A Pinot Noir from Burgundy

Open Pithiviers of Kohlrabi, Potato and Cauliflower with Paprika Sauce

In a classic pithiviers the filling is baked in the pastry but in my version the vegetables are cooked separately and then piled into the pastry cases just before serving.

450g/1lb puff pastry
1 egg beaten with 1 tbsp milk or water, to glaze

FOR THE PAPRIKA SAUCE
1 shallot, finely chopped
1 small clove garlic, crushed
1 small red pepper, roughly chopped
1 ripe tomato, deseeded and chopped
25g/1oz unsalted butter
1 tsp paprika
1 tsp caraway seeds
90ml/3fl oz dry white wine
1 tsp tomato purée
200ml/7fl oz vegetable stock (see page 148)
125ml/4fl oz double cream, semi-whipped

FOR THE FILLING
225g/8oz kohlrabi, cut into 1cm/ ½ inch dice
225g/8oz potato, cut into 1cm/ ½ inch dice
12 cauliflower florets
½ red pepper, cut into 1cm/½ inch dice
25g/1oz unsalted butter
1 tbsp extra virgin olive oil
½ tsp crushed garlic
2 tsp paprika
1 tsp caraway seeds
salt and freshly ground black pepper
100ml/3½fl oz vegetable stock (see page 148)

Preheat the oven to 180°C (350°F, Gas Mark 4). To prepare the pithiviers cases, roll out the pastry approximately 1cm/½ inch thick and cut out 4 rounds with a 13cm/5 inch fluted or plain cutter. With a small kitchen knife, cut small slashes radiating in an arc shape from the centre of each pastry round to the edges. Place the pastry rounds on a buttered baking sheet, brush with the beaten egg and chill in the refrigerator for up to 15 minutes. Remove and brush with a second coating of egg, then bake in the preheated oven for 15–20 minutes, until golden brown; remove from the oven and keep warm.

To make the sauce, sweat the shallot, garlic, red pepper and tomato in the butter until softened. Stir in the paprika, caraway seeds and wine and boil rapidly until the wine is reduced by half its original volume. Add the tomato purée and simmer for 3–4 minutes. Stir in the vegetable stock, bring to the boil and skim off any impurities on the surface, then reduce the heat and simmer gently for 10–15 minutes. Blend in a liquidizer or food processor until smooth, then pass the sauce through a fine sieve and set aside.

To make the filling, blanch all the vegetables separately in a large pan of boiling salted water for 1 minute and then drain. Heat the butter and oil in a pan, add the garlic, paprika and caraway seeds and cook for 1 minute, then stir in the blanched vegetables. Season to taste and pour on the stock. Cover and cook until tender.

Just before serving, bring the sauce back to the boil, then take it off the heat and whisk the semi-whipped cream into it until frothy.

To serve, cut the pastry cases in half horizontally and carefully remove the uncooked pastry within. Arrange the vegetables in the pastry bases and put them on serving plates. Coat each one with the paprika sauce and top with the pastry lids. Serve at once, with any remaining sauce.

WINE NOTES

An Australian Cabernet Sauvignon

*O*pen Pithiviers of Kohlrabi, Potato and
Cauliflower with Paprika Sauce

Creole Spiced Vegetable Fritters with Lemon Sauce

This recipe is suitable for other vegetables, too, such as okra and asparagus.

vegetable oil, for deep-frying
2 aubergines, cut into slices 1cm/
½ inch thick, salted for 15 minutes, then rinsed and drained
1 small cauliflower, divided into florets, blanched and refreshed
2 courgettes, cut into slices 1cm/
½ inch thick
450g/1lb broccoli, divided into florets, blanched and refreshed
2 beetroot, cooked, peeled and cut into wedges
50g/2oz French beans, blanched and refreshed

FOR THE LEMON SAUCE
zest and juice of 1 lemon
5 tbsp crème fraîche or soured cream
1 tbsp chopped coriander leaves
½ tsp creole mustard (optional)

FOR THE BATTER
250g/9oz plain flour
250ml/8fl oz iced water
2 tbsp olive oil
salt and freshly ground black pepper
2 egg whites

FOR THE CREOLE SEASONING
1 red chilli, deseeded and chopped
1 clove garlic, crushed
a pinch of freshly ground black pepper
1 tbsp chopped parsley
1 tbsp thyme leaves

First make the lemon sauce by stirring together all the ingredients in a bowl. Set it aside and make the batter. Sieve the flour into a bowl, add the water, oil and seasoning and beat until smooth. In a separate bowl, whisk the egg whites until stiff and then fold them into the batter (don't do this until you are ready to use the batter or it will drop).

In a large saucepan, heat some oil for deep-frying to about 160°C/325°F. Dip the prepared vegetables into the batter and fry them in the hot oil a few at a time for about 2 minutes, until golden and crisp. They should be cooked *al dente*. Drain the fritters on kitchen paper to remove excess grease and keep them warm while you fry the remaining vegetables

For the creole seasoning, heat a frying pan, add the chilli, garlic and black pepper and fry for 30 seconds until they give off their fragrance. Add the vegetable fritters to the pan and toss the whole lot together for a few minutes. Finally add the parsley and the thyme and serve straight away, accompanied by the lemon sauce.

WINE NOTES

A spicy Spanish white, such as an Alvariño

Roasted Carrot and Tarragon Purée

I came up with the idea of roasting vegetables and turning them into a delicious purée quite by accident when a private function was cancelled at the last moment, leaving a garnish of roasted vegetables to go to waste. I now prepare roasted vegetable purées on a regular basis. Here are some of my favourites; other root vegetables, such as Jerusalem artichokes, swede and sweet potatoes, also work well.

15g/½oz tarragon leaves
4 tbsp vegetable oil
450g/1lb small new-season carrots, peeled and cut into 1cm/½ inch dice
salt and freshly ground black pepper
50g/2oz unsalted butter
4 tbsp single cream

Preheat the oven to 180°C (350°F, Gas Mark 4). Blanch the tarragon leaves in a small pan of boiling water for 10 seconds, then drain through a sieve, refresh in iced water, drain again and dry. Set aside.

Heat the oil in an ovenproof casserole, add the carrots and season lightly with salt. Cook for 2–3 minutes until pale golden, turning them frequently, then transfer the dish to the preheated oven and cook, uncovered, for 20–25 minutes, until the carrots are golden and tender. Add half the butter and cook for a further 5 minutes until they are a beautiful deep golden brown colour. Roasted in this way, the carrots give off their natural sugars, which produce a wonderful caramelized flavour.

Transfer the roasted carrots to a food processor or a liquidizer, add the tarragon and blitz to a smooth purée with a little of the cream, scraping down the sides of the bowl to ensure no small bits remain in the purée.

Add the remaining cream and butter, season with salt and pepper and serve. The purée can be made several hours in advance and reheated gently just before serving.

VARIATIONS
ROASTED CELERIAC PURÉE

Substitute peeled and diced celeriac for the carrots and omit the tarragon.

ROASTED PARSNIP AND ROOT GINGER PURÉE

Omit the tarragon. Substitute peeled and diced parsnips for the carrots and add 15g/½oz fresh ginger root, thinly sliced, with the first half of the butter.

N.V.
Suggestion

All vegetable purées are excellent with game, such as venison or grouse.

Courgette Fritters

100g/4oz green courgettes
100g/4oz yellow courgettes
salt and freshly ground black pepper
50g/2oz plain flour
3 egg yolks
1 tbsp milk
clarified butter (see page 151) or olive
oil, for frying

Coarsely grate the courgettes, then place them on a tray or in a colander, sprinkle with salt and leave for 30 minutes to extract the excess moisture. Wash thoroughly under cold running water, then drain and dry well.

Put the courgettes in a bowl and mix in the flour, egg yolks and milk. Season to taste.

Pour a thin film of clarified butter or oil into a large frying pan over a moderate heat. When it is hot, drop in 4 tablespoonfuls of the courgette mixture to make 4 fritters. Cook for 1 minute until golden underneath, then turn over and cook the other side. Remove from the pan and drain on paper towels. Repeat with the remaining mixture – you should have 8 fritters in all. Serve immediately.

WINE NOTES

An oaky American Chardonnay

Sweet and Sour Peperonata

A sweet and sour version of the classic Italian dish. Black olives can be included, for a change.

2 tbsp extra virgin olive oil
450g/1lb mixed peppers (red, green and
yellow), cut into strips
salt and freshly ground black pepper
1 celery stick, cut into slices 5mm/
¼ inch thick
1 onion, chopped
2 cloves garlic, crushed
25g/1oz raisins
1 bay leaf
4 tbsp sherry vinegar
4 tbsp honey
175ml/6fl oz water
2 plum tomatoes, peeled, deseeded and
cut into strips

Heat the olive oil in a frying pan, add the peppers and season lightly. Cook gently for 5–10 minutes, then stir in all the remaining ingredients except the tomatoes and bring to the boil. Reduce the heat and simmer for 10–15 minutes or until the peppers are very tender. Stir in the tomatoes, remove from the heat and adjust the seasoning. Serve cold.

N.V. Suggestion

Marinate some fresh scallops overnight in a little olive oil and some herbs, then grill them and serve with the peperonata.

Baked Sweet and Sour Red Onions

325g/12oz red onions
50g/2oz caster sugar
300ml/½ pint red wine
200ml/7fl oz red wine vinegar
90ml/3fl oz grenadine
25g/1oz unsalted butter
90ml/3fl oz extra virgin olive oil
salt and freshly ground black pepper

Preheat the oven to 180°C (350°F, Gas Mark 4). Peel the onions, leaving the root end intact, then cut them in half vertically. Place them cut-side down on a chopping board and cut in 5mm/¼ inch thick slices through the root.

Put the sugar, red wine, vinegar and grenadine in a saucepan and bring to the boil. Heat the butter and oil in an ovenproof casserole, add the onion wedges and stir gently until they are coated in the oil. Pour on the wine and vinegar mixture and season lightly. Cover and bake in the preheated oven for 15–20 minutes, until the onions are tender and the liquid has completely evaporated. Serve warm or cold.

Green Beans with Mushrooms, Balsamic Vinegar and Roasted Onions

100g/4oz button onions, peeled
3 tbsp vegetable oil
2 tbsp demerara sugar
50g/2oz unsalted butter
6 tbsp balsamic vinegar
150ml/¼ pint Dark Vegetable Stock (see page 148)
325g/12oz French beans, topped and tailed
100g/4oz button mushrooms, sliced
salt and freshly ground black pepper

Preheat the oven to 200°C (400°F, Gas Mark 6). Blanch the button onions in a pan of boiling salted water for 1 minute, then drain well.

Heat the oil in a roasting pan on the hob, add the onions and cook over a moderate to high heat until golden brown. Then add the sugar, butter and vinegar and cook until the onions are caramelized. Pour in the stock, turn the onions to coat them with the liquid, then transfer the dish to the preheated oven.

Meanwhile, cook the French beans in a pan of boiling salted water for 3–4 minutes, until just tender. Drain them in a colander and add to the onions, together with the mushrooms; season and mix well together. Return the dish to the oven for about 10 minutes, until the onions are cooked, then serve immediately.

WINE NOTES

A young Hungarian Cabernet Sauvignon

*B*raised Beetroot, Green Beans with Mushrooms, Balsamic Vinegar
and Roasted Onions (page 115), and Red Wine-Glazed Turnips

Braised Beetroot

In this recipe beetroot is prepared in the Flemish style, like red cabbage. I sometimes like to add a little orange zest to give another dimension.

450g/1lb raw beetroot, peeled
90ml/3fl oz red wine
4 tbsp red wine vinegar
1 tbsp sugar
125g/4½oz unsalted butter, cut into small pieces
salt and freshly ground black pepper
1 tbsp redcurrant jelly

Preheat the oven to 180°C (350°F, Gas Mark 4). Cut the beetroot into fine strips with a sharp knife or a mandoline, or alternatively use a food processor fitted with a coarse grating blade. Place the beetroot in an ovenproof dish, add the red wine, vinegar, sugar and butter, season lightly and cover with a tight-fitting lid. Bake in the preheated oven, stirring occasionally, for 25–30 minutes, until the beetroot is cooked through. Adjust the seasoning to taste, mix in the redcurrant jelly to form a light glaze around the beetroot, and serve.

> ### N.V.
> #### Suggestion
>
> **Excellent with roasted game birds such as pheasant.**

Red Wine-Glazed Turnips

450g/1lb baby turnips, scraped clean but tops left on
150ml/¼ pint red wine
20g/¾oz caster sugar
25g/1oz unsalted butter, cut into small pieces
salt and freshly ground black pepper

Place the turnips in a small shallow saucepan so they fit in a single layer, pour in the red wine and top up with cold water just to cover the turnips. Add the sugar, butter and some salt.

Bring to the boil, then reduce the heat and cook gently until the turnips are tender. Remove the turnips from the pan with a slotted spoon, increase the heat to high and cook until the liquid has reduced enough to form a glaze. Return the turnips to the glaze and turn them in it to coat. Adjust the seasoning and serve.

Haricot Beans with Dill and Anise

300g/11oz haricot beans, soaked overnight and then drained
1 small carrot, thickly sliced
1 small onion cloute (see page 149)
1 clove garlic, halved
25g/1oz softened unsalted butter
25g/1oz plain flour
4 tbsp Tomato Concassée (see page 151)
2 tsp Pernod
2 tbsp chopped dill
salt and freshly ground black pepper

Place the soaked haricot beans in a large saucepan, add the carrot, onion cloute and garlic and cover with cold water. Bring to the boil, then reduce the heat and simmer for about 1 hour or until the beans are tender, adding more water if necessary. Drain the beans, reserving their cooking liquid. Remove the vegetables from the beans and discard them.

Blend the butter and flour together to form a smooth paste. Bring 300ml/½ pint of the cooking liquid to the boil in a clean pan and thicken it by whisking in the butter and flour mixture a little at a time (you may not need it all), until it is thick enough to coat the back of a spoon. Cook for 2 minutes, then strain into a clean pan. Stir the beans into the sauce, then add the tomato concassée, Pernod and dill. Season to taste and serve.

> ### N.V.
> #### Suggestion
> ----
> **Serve as an accompaniment to roast duck or grilled lamb cutlets.**

Potato and Rocket Gratin

1 clove garlic, peeled
25g/1oz unsalted butter
50g/2oz rocket leaves
salt and freshly ground black pepper
675g/1½lb baking potatoes, thinly sliced
freshly grated nutmeg
600ml/1 pint double cream
50g/2oz Gruyère or Emmenthal cheese, grated (optional)

Preheat the oven to 180°C (350°F, Gas Mark 4). Cut the garlic clove in half, flatten it with a knife, then rub it round a 25cm/10 inch gratin dish; reserve the garlic. Grease the dish liberally with 15g/½oz of the butter. Heat the remaining butter in a pan, add the rocket leaves, cook for 1 minute until wilted and then season.

Arrange the potatoes in neat layers in the dish, adding some rocket between each layer and seasoning generously with nutmeg, salt and pepper as you go.

Meanwhile, bring the cream to the boil in a pan with the garlic. Leave to infuse for 2–3 minutes, then strain it on to the gratin, ensuring that the liquid covers the potatoes (top up with milk if necessary). Sprinkle with the cheese, if using, and bake in the preheated oven for about 40–45 minutes until the potatoes are tender and the top is golden brown.

Twice-cooked Sweet Potatoes with Gremolata

Sweet potatoes are very good baked in the oven, then split open and filled with plain or herb-flavoured butter but if you have a little more time, try preparing them this way. You really do need a barbecue so it's an ideal recipe for the summer.

4 sweet potatoes
4 tbsp extra virgin olive oil
coarse sea salt

FOR THE GREMOLATA
1 tsp grated lemon zest
1 small clove garlic, crushed
2 tbsp chopped flat-leaf parsley

Preheat the oven to 200°C (400°F, Gas Mark 6). Prick the sweet potatoes all over with a small sharp knife. Place them on a baking tray and bake for 40 minutes, until they are just tender but not too soft – if you cook them for too long they will fall apart when you slice them.

Leave the potatoes to cool, then slice them into 2cm/¾ inch rounds. Brush them with the olive oil, season with salt and grill on a charcoal grill until golden and caramelized in colour. Mix together the ingredients for the gremolata, sprinkle it over the potatoes and serve.

> ### N.V.
> #### Suggestion
>
> Try topping the potatoes with some crispy sautéed lardons of bacon.

Old-Fashioned Baked Leeks with Mustard

Salsify can be cooked in the same way.

1 tsp caster sugar
8 medium leeks, trimmed
15g/½oz unsalted butter
1 tbsp plain flour
300ml/½ pint vegetable stock (see page 148)
2 tbsp mild Dijon mustard
150ml /¼ pint double cream (optional)
salt and freshly ground black pepper

Preheat the oven to 180°C (350°F, Gas Mark 4). Bring a large pan of salted water to the boil and add the sugar. Plunge the leeks into the water, lower the heat and simmer for 4–5 minutes. Drain and reserve the cooking liquid.

Heat the butter in a small pan, stir in the flour and cook over a gentle heat for 1–2 minutes. Gradually add 300ml/½ pint of the reserved cooking liquid, then add the vegetable stock, stirring constantly. Bring to the boil, stirring constantly, and cook for 10 minutes over a low heat. Stir in the mustard and the cream, if using, and season to taste.

Arrange the leeks in an ovenproof dish and season with salt and pepper. Coat the leeks with the sauce, bake in the preheated oven for 10 minutes, then serve.

> ### N.V.
> #### Suggestion
>
> Wrap the leeks in ham or smoked bacon before coating with the sauce.

Puddings, Granitas and Sorbets

Our love of puddings and desserts has never faltered over the years; even in these days of dieting and healthy living. In this chapter, you will find some desserts that are simple and easy to prepare, and others that require a little more time and involvement, but which will be well worth the end result.

I have tried to show the versatility of vegetables with a selection of vegetable-based desserts, such as Pumpkin and Orange Brûlée, Plum Tomato and Ricotta Fool and Fennel Sorbet. The advantage of granitas, sorbets, and ice creams is that they can be made ahead and kept in the freezer until required. The ices can be served as a dessert or as a palate cleanser between courses in a formal meal.

Chocolate and Prune Pudding with Coffee and White Bean Ice-Cream

The beauty of this dessert is that the pudding mixture may be made 1–2 days in advance, put into the flan rings, then kept in the fridge and baked when needed.

¼ tsp fresh yeast
100g/4oz good-quality plain chocolate
100g/4oz softened unsalted butter
75g/3oz caster sugar
2 eggs
75g/3oz self-raising flour
2 level dsp cornflour
8 prunes, preferably Agen prunes, soaked
in tea overnight and then drained
125ml/4fl oz Vanilla Custard Sauce
(see page 151)
a few chocolate-coated coffee beans, to
decorate (optional)

FOR THE ICE-CREAM
175g/6oz white haricot beans, soaked
overnight and then drained
100ml/3½fl oz water
190g/6½oz caster sugar
250ml/8fl oz milk
250ml/8fl oz double cream
6 egg yolks
1 tsp Camp coffee extract
2 tbsp rum

FOR THE CHOCOLATE SAUCE
50g/2oz good-quality plain chocolate
40g/1½oz caster sugar
100ml/3½fl oz water

First make the ice-cream. Put the white beans in a pan, cover with water and cook over a gentle heat for 1–1½ hours until very soft. Drain the beans and place in a clean pan; add the water and 50g/2oz of the sugar and cook for a further 5 minutes to sweeten them. Transfer them to a food processor and blitz to a fine purée.

Put the milk, double cream and half the remaining sugar in a saucepan and bring to the boil, then remove from the heat. In a bowl, cream the egg yolks with all the remaining sugar. Gently pour in the hot milk mixture, stirring all the time, then pour this back into the pan and cook over a very low heat until the mixture thickens, stirring constantly with a wooden spoon until the custard is thick enough to coat the back of it. Don't let it boil or it will curdle.

Remove the custard from the heat and stir in the bean purée, coffee extract and rum. Strain, then leave to cool (it can be kept in the refrigerator for up to 12 hours at this stage). Pour the mixture into an ice-cream maker and process according to the manufacturer's instructions. If you don't have an ice-cream maker, pour the mixture into a bowl and put it in the freezer. After about 30 minutes, when the mixture is beginning to set, remove it from the freezer and beat well with an electric beater or hand whisk to disperse any ice crystals, then return it to the freezer. Repeat this 2 or 3 times until the ice-cream is set firm.

For the pudding, preheat the oven to 160°C (325°F, Gas Mark 3). Mix the yeast with 2 teaspoons of warm water and set aside until it begins to froth. Melt the chocolate in a bowl set over a pan of hot water. Cool slightly, then mix in the butter and sugar. Beat in the eggs, one at a time and then stir in the yeast. Finally sieve the flour and cornflour and gently fold them into the mixture.

Lightly butter four 6–8cm/2½–3 inch deep flan rings (or ramekins), set them on a baking tray and half fill them with the chocolate mixture. Place 2 prunes in the centre of each one, then top with the remaining mixture. Bake in the preheated oven for about 12–15 minutes. To test whether the puddings are cooked, insert a small knife into the centre of one to see if it comes out clean; if it is a little gooey, cook for a further 4 minutes. Remove from the oven and leave to cool.

To make the chocolate sauce, put all the ingredients in a pan and heat gently to dissolve the sugar. Then bring to the boil, stirring all the time.

To serve, unmould the chocolate puddings on to plates and spoon the vanilla custard sauce around. Top with a scoop of ice-cream, drizzle with the chocolate sauce and decorate with chocolate-coated coffee beans, if liked. Serve immediately.

*C*hocolate and Prune Pudding with Coffee and White Bean Ice-Cream, and
Iced Lemon Parfait with Kadaifi and Warm Cherry Compote (page 124)

Iced Lemon Parfait with Kadaifi and Warm Cherry Compote

Kadaifi, or kataifi as it is also known, is used in Greek dishes and is a type of shredded wheat pastry similar to filo. It is available from Greek and Middle Eastern groceries and can be kept in the freezer.

125g/4½oz caster sugar
100ml/3½fl oz water
zest and juice of 2 small lemons
5 egg yolks
200ml/7fl oz double cream, semi-whipped
150g/5oz kadaifi
75g/3oz butter, melted
50g/2oz icing sugar, plus extra for dusting
sprigs of mint, to decorate

FOR THE CHERRY COMPOTE
450g/1lb black cherries, stoned
75g/3oz caster sugar
1 tsp lemon juice
1 tsp lemon zest
a little kirsch, to taste

To make the parfait, put the caster sugar, water and lemon zest in a pan, bring to the boil and cook until it reaches 110–115°C on a sugar thermometer (soft ball stage).

Beat the egg yolks in a food processor with a whisk attachment or in a bowl with an electric mixer until they double in volume. Keeping the machine running, pour the hot syrup on to the yolks, add the lemon juice and continue whisking until the mixture is cold and quite aerated. Gently fold in the double cream with a metal spoon. Pour the mixture into four 6cm/2½ inch flan rings placed on a tray (or use ramekins), then level the tops and place in the freezer.

For the kadaifi, preheat the oven to 180°C (350°F, Gas Mark 4). Unwrap the dough and put it in a bowl, unravelling it slightly as you do so. Add the melted butter and icing sugar and gently work them through the dough with your fingers until it is well coated. Divide the kadaifi into 8 portions and use a pastry cutter to shape them into rounds slightly wider than the parfaits. Place them on a baking sheet and bake in the preheated oven for about 8–10 minutes, until lightly golden, then leave to cool.

For the cherry compote, place 150g/5oz of the cherries in a liquidizer and blitz to a pulp. Strain the pulp, then transfer it to a pan, add the sugar and 4 tablespoons of water and boil until the sugar has dissolved. Add the remaining cherries and poach gently for 1–2 minutes. Stir in the lemon juice and zest and the kirsch.

To assemble the dessert, place a cooked kadaifi round on each serving plate. Turn out the lemon parfaits by sliding a knife around the edges and dipping them briefly in hot water. Place a lemon parfait on top of each kadaifi round, then top with the remaining kaidafi and dust with icing sugar. Pour the warm cherry compote around them, decorate with mint and serve immediately.

WINE NOTES

A Sauternes or Barsac such as Château Broustet

Apricot Frangipane Tart with Mascarpone

1 quantity of Basic Sweet Pastry (see page 155)
15 fresh apricots, halved and stoned
125g/4½oz ground almonds
125g/4½oz softened unsalted butter
125g/4½oz caster sugar
2 tbsp apricot brandy (optional)
1 egg
4 tbsp apricot jam
icing sugar, for dusting
150g/5oz mascarpone cheese

FOR POACHING THE APRICOTS
400ml/14fl oz water
200g/7oz caster sugar
½ vanilla pod, split

Preheat the oven to 180°C (350°F, Gas Mark 4). Roll out the pastry and use to line a deep 20cm/8 inch tart tin. Line with greaseproof paper, fill with cooking beans and bake blind for 8–10 minutes. Remove the paper and beans and return to the oven for 5 minutes, then leave to cool. Leave the oven on.

Put all the ingredients for poaching the apricots in a pan, bring to the boil and simmer gently for a few minutes until the sugar has dissolved. Add the apricot halves and poach them on a gentle simmer for 4–5 minutes. Remove the apricots with a slotted spoon and leave to cool.

To make the frangipane, put the ground almonds, butter, sugar and apricot brandy, if using, in a bowl or an electric mixer and beat until well creamed, then beat in the egg. Chill for 30 minutes.

Spread the base of the pastry case with the jam, then half fill it with the frangipane (there may be a little left over; use to make individual tarts). Arrange the apricot halves on top, then bake in the preheated oven for 30–35 minutes, until golden. Remove the tart from the oven and cool slightly before dusting with icing sugar. Serve warm with the mascarpone cheese.

Tempura Fruit Salad with Lemon Grass Sorbet

It's important to choose fruit that is perfectly ripe for the tempura.

1 papaya
1 mango
100g/4oz fresh pineapple
2 bananas
8 physalis
8 strawberries
vegetable oil, for frying
plain flour and icing sugar, for dusting
Lemon Grass Sorbet (see page 137)

FOR THE BATTER
1 egg yolk
250ml/8fl oz iced water
250g/9oz plain flour
1 tsp caster sugar

To make the batter, put the egg yolk and water in a bowl and gently mix in the flour and sugar. It should be a little lumpy; if it is smooth the batter has been overworked. Place to one side while preparing the fruit.

Peel the papaya, mango, pineapple and bananas and cut them into cubes or wedges as required. Lift the outer husk off the physalis but do not remove it. Cut the strawberries in half vertically, leaving the stalks attached.

Heat the vegetable oil in a deep-fryer or saucepan to a temperature of 180°C/350°F. Dust the fruits with a little flour, then dip them into the batter. Fry in the hot oil for 1–2 minutes until crisp and golden, turning them occasionally. Drain the fruit on kitchen paper, dust with icing sugar and arrange in serving dishes. Serve immediately, accompanied by the sorbet.

*S*now Eggs with Caramelized Pears and Saffron Custard,
and Passion Fruit Soufflé Gratin (page 128)

Snow Eggs with Caramelized Pears and Saffron Custard

5 egg whites
175g/6oz caster sugar
75g/3oz icing sugar
500ml/18fl oz milk
2 vanilla pods, split lengthways
2 tbsp flaked almonds, toasted

FOR THE SAFFRON CUSTARD
150ml/¼ pint double cream
a pinch of saffron strands
2 egg yolks
25g/1oz caster sugar

FOR THE CARAMELIZED PEARS
4 Williams pears
200g/7oz caster sugar
250ml/8fl oz orange juice

FOR THE CARAMEL TOPPING
4 tbsp water
125g/4½oz caster sugar

For the snow eggs, put the egg whites and half the caster sugar in a deep bowl and place it over a pan of hot water. Whisk vigorously for 3–4 minutes to warm the egg whites and dissolve the sugar. Remove from the pan of hot water and whisk with an electric beater until the whites are stiff and stand in peaks. Using a large metal spoon, fold in the remaining caster sugar and the icing sugar.

Bring the milk and vanilla pods to the boil in a large shallow pan, then reduce the heat and simmer for 5 minutes. Using 2 tablespoons or a wet ice-cream scoop, mould 12 meringues from the egg white mixture (or pipe the meringues using a piping bag fitted with a 1cm/½ inch nozzle). Gently lower them into the simmering milk and poach for 2 minutes, then remove with a slotted spoon and place on a clean cloth to drain. Cool and then refrigerate.

To make the saffron custard you will need 150ml/¼ pint of the milk from poaching the meringues. Put this milk in a saucepan with the cream and saffron, bring to the boil, then remove from the heat and leave to infuse for a few minutes. Beat the egg yolks and sugar together in a bowl, then pour on the warm cream mixture, stirring all the time. Return this mixture to the saucepan and cook over a very gentle heat, stirring constantly, until the custard is thick enough to coat the back of the spoon; don't let it boil or it will curdle. When it has thickened, remove from the heat and leave to cool, then refrigerate.

To make the caramelized pears, peel the pears and, using a melon baller, scoop out pear balls (or alternatively cut the pears into wedges). Put the sugar in a heavy-based pan and melt it over a low heat until it is just turning golden, watching it carefully to make sure it doesn't burn. Add the orange juice and the pears to the caramelized sugar (stand well back as the mixture will flare up and splatter) and cook over a high heat for 3–4 minutes, until the pears are tender and caramelized. Remove the pears from the pan with a slotted spoon and leave to cool.

For the caramel topping, put 4 tablespoons of water into a straight-sided, heavy-based pan, then add the sugar, bring to the boil and cook until it becomes a rich caramel, about 2 minutes. Place the hot pan into a container of iced water to arrest the cooking process and leave to cool for about a minute until the mixture becomes tacky. Dip a fork in the syrup and spin it in vertical and then horizontal lines on a sheet of baking parchment. Leave for 5–10 minutes until it becomes brittle. Break the caramel into large pieces to decorate the snow eggs.

To serve, pour the chilled saffron custard into a serving bowl, place the snow eggs on top and decorate with the pears, toasted almonds and caramel. Serve chilled.

WINE NOTES

A Sauternes or Barsac such as Château Broustet

Passion Fruit Soufflé Gratin

200ml/7fl oz milk
150g/5oz caster sugar
¼ vanilla pod, split
65g/2½oz unsalted butter
65g/2½oz plain flour
4 eggs, separated
juice of 8 passion fruit, strained
100g/4oz fresh raspberries
sprigs of mint, to decorate
a little icing sugar, for dusting

FOR THE SABAYON
4 egg yolks
50g/2oz caster sugar
1½ tbsp kirsch
2 tbsp double cream, very lightly whipped

Preheat the oven to 180°C (350°F, Gas Mark 4). To make the soufflé, put the milk, 50g/2oz of the caster sugar and the vanilla pod into a pan, bring to the boil and leave to infuse for 3–4 minutes. Strain to remove the vanilla pod.

Melt the butter in a small pan, stir in the flour and cook over a low heat for 1–2 minutes. Gradually add the milk and sugar mixture, stirring well to avoid any lumps, and cook until it forms a thick sauce. Cook for a further 3–4 minutes, remove from the heat and leave to cool.

Add the egg yolks and passion fruit juice to the mixture. Meanwhile, beat the egg whites and the remaining sugar with a hand whisk or an electric mixer until stiff. Beat a quarter of the whites into the egg yolk mixture and then gently fold in the remaining egg white with a metal spoon.

Butter four 200ml/7fl oz ramekins and lightly dust with a little caster sugar. Fill them three-quarters full with the soufflé mixture, then place in a roasting tin and pour hot water into the tin to come at least halfway up the sides of the dishes. Bake in the preheated oven for up to 20 minutes, until risen and lightly set.

Meanwhile, make the sabayon. Place the egg yolks, sugar, kirsch and 1 tablespoon of water in a large bowl and place it over a pan of simmering water. Whisk until the mixture increases to 3–4 times its original vol-ume – this will take a good 5 minutes with an electric hand mixer and longer with a whisk. Continue whisking until the mixture thickens but do not let it boil. Remove from the heat and gently fold in the cream.

To serve, remove the soufflés from the oven, leave for 2–3 minutes, then unmould on to a serving dish. Coat them with the sabayon sauce and return to the oven for 3–4 minutes, until golden brown, or place them under a hot grill for 1 minute. Decorate with the raspberries and mint, dust with icing sugar and serve immediately.

WINE NOTES

A late-harvested New Zealand Riesling such as Redwood Valley

Quince or Pear Tatin with Ginger Caramel and Cardamom Ice-Cream

By all means use bought puff pastry for this recipe; it is worth trying to find one that has been made with butter.

FOR THE TATIN
200g/7oz puff pastry
40g/1½oz unsalted butter
75g/3oz caster sugar
40g/1½oz stem ginger, finely diced
2 large quinces or 4 Williams pears, preferably pink ones
1 egg beaten with 1 tbsp milk or water, to glaze
sprigs of mint, to decorate (optional)

FOR THE CARDAMOM ICE-CREAM
250ml/8fl oz milk
250ml/8fl oz double cream
½ tbsp cardamom seeds, crushed
zest of ½ orange
200g/7oz caster sugar
6 egg yolks

First make the cardamom ice-cream. Put the milk, double cream, cardamom seeds, orange zest and half the sugar in a saucepan and bring to the boil, then remove from the heat. Cream the egg yolks with the remaining sugar in a bowl, then pour on the hot cream mixture, stirring all the time. Pour this back into the pan and cook over a very low heat, stirring constantly with a wooden spoon, until the custard is thick enough to coat the back of the spoon. On no account let it boil.

When the custard has thickened, remove it from the heat and strain, then leave to cool. Pour it into an ice-cream maker and freeze according to the manufacturer's instructions. If you don't have an ice-cream maker, pour the ice-cream into a bowl and place it in the freezer. After about 30 minutes, when the mixture is beginning to set, remove it from the freezer and beat it with an electric beater or hand whisk to disperse any ice crystals. Repeat this 2 or 3 times until the ice-cream is firm.

Preheat the oven to 200°C (400°F, Gas Mark 6). Roll out the puff pastry and cut out from it a circle 23cm/9 inches in diameter, using a plate or a tin as a guide.

Take a heavy-based cast-iron frying pan, 20cm/8 inches in diameter and suitable for use in the oven. Smear it well with the butter and sprinkle on the sugar and stem ginger. Peel and core the quinces or pears and cut them into large wedges. Arrange them in concentric circles in the frying pan until the base is completely covered, then place the pan over a very high heat and cook until the sugar and butter are caramelized to a light golden colour. Remove from the heat and allow to cool slightly before covering the fruit with the pastry circle. Press the pastry down, tucking it over the fruit at the edges, brush with a little beaten egg and then bake in the preheated oven for about 15 minutes, until the pastry is risen and golden. About every 5 minutes, press down on the pastry with a plate or another pan the same size as the frying pan.

When the tatin is cooked, remove it from the oven and turn it out on to a plate: to do this, place a plate on top and, holding the plate and the handle of the frying pan together (remembering that the handle will be very hot!), carefully invert the pan so that the tart is released on to the plate. Pour any ginger caramel that is left in the pan over the tart. Decorate with the mint, if using, and serve immediately with the ice-cream.

129

Pumpkin and Orange Brûlée with Orange Compote

In order to caramelize the brûlée you need a small domestic blow torch – a useful, if unexpected, kitchen accessory.

FOR THE BRULEE
200g/7oz caster sugar
300ml /½ pint water
400g/14oz pumpkin, peeled and diced
125ml/4fl oz milk
125ml/4fl oz double cream
zest and juice of 2 oranges
4 eggs
4 egg yolks
8 tbsp demerara sugar

FOR THE ORANGE COMPOTE
6 oranges
½ tsp finely grated fresh ginger root
1 tbsp caster sugar
1 tsp arrowroot
2 tbsp Grand Marnier or Cointreau

SERVES 8

Preheat the oven to 160°C (325°F, Gas Mark 3). Put 150g/5oz of the caster sugar in a saucepan with the water and boil until it forms a light syrup. Add the pumpkin, reduce the heat and cook gently until soft. Transfer to a food processor or liquidizer and blitz to a smooth purée.

Put the milk, cream and half the remaining caster sugar in a pan with the orange zest and juice and bring to the boil, then remove from the heat and cool slightly. Cream the eggs and yolks with the remaining sugar in a bowl, then pour on the hot cream mixture, stirring all the time. Next stir in the pumpkin purée, pass the mixture through a fine strainer and pour it into 8 individual ramekins, about 175ml/ 6fl oz each in capacity.

Place the dishes in a baking tin and pour in enough boiling water to come half way up the sides. Bake in the preheated oven for 30 minutes or until just set. Remove and leave to cool.

To make the orange compote, use a zester to remove the zest from all the oranges in fine strips. Blanch the zest in a small pan of boiling water for 1 minute; drain and refresh under cold running water, then transfer it to a bowl. Peel and segment 4 of the oranges (see page 47), reserving the juice and adding the segments to the bowl containing the orange zest. Squeeze the juice from the remaining 2 oranges.

Pour all the orange juice into a small pan, add the ginger and sugar and bring to the boil. Simmer for 1 minute, then mix the arrowroot with the Grand Marnier or Cointreau and stir it into the pan. Cook for 1 minute until slightly thickened. Pour this orange sauce over the orange zest and segments and leave to cool.

Shortly before serving, sprinkle 2 tablespoons of demerara sugar over each pumpkin custard and clean the rim of the dishes to remove any excess sugar. Use a small blow torch to glaze the sugar: hold the torch about 4cm/1½ inches away from the surface of each custard and pass it back and forth until the sugar begins to bubble and caramelize. Take care not to get it too close or the sugar may burn; it should just form a crispy, golden brown crust. Leave to cool to room temperature but do not refrigerate.

To serve, place each ramekin dish on a plate and spoon a little orange compote to the side.

WINE NOTES

An Australian Muscat such as Brown Brothers

*P*ear Tatin with Ginger Caramel and Cardamom Ice-Cream (page 129),
and Pumpkin and Orange Brûlée with Orange Compote

Goat's Cheese and Pineapple Mousse with Blackcurrant Sauce

In this recipe goat's cheese is transformed into a delicious dessert.

1 small pineapple
300ml/½ pint water
200g/7oz caster sugar
600g/1lb 6 oz mild fresh goat's cheese
200g/7oz icing sugar
250ml/8fl oz double cream, semi-whipped

FOR THE BLACKCURRANT SAUCE
200g/7oz fresh or frozen blackcurrants, plus extra to decorate
juice of 1 orange
a little sugar, to taste

SERVES 6–8

Remove the outer skin of the pineapple and cut the flesh into rings, then remove the hard central core. Put the water and sugar in a pan and bring to the boil to make a syrup. Add the pineapple, reduce the heat and simmer gently for about 45–50 minutes, until the pineapple becomes tacky and candied in appearance. Leave to cool in the syrup. (This can be prepared well in advance.)

Put the goat's cheese and icing sugar in a food processor and process until smooth, then transfer to a bowl. Drain the pineapple well and leave it to dry, then cut it into very small dice and add to the cheese. Gently fold in the double cream. Place the mixture in the fridge to firm up for at least 4 hours or overnight.

To make the sauce, put the blackcurrants in a blender with the orange juice and sugar and blitz to a smooth purée. Strain through a fine sieve.

Either serve the mousse in a large glass bowl and hand round the blackcurrant sauce separately or shape it into quenelles with 2 tablespoons, arrange them on serving plates and pour round the sauce. Decorate with blackcurrants.

WINE NOTES

A late-harvested Tokay or Gewürztraminer from Alsace

Plum Tomato and Ricotta Fool

Tomato is a fruit and its natural sweetness is emphasized in this unusual and attractive layered dessert.

FOR THE TOMATO CREAM
225g/8oz caster sugar
3 tbsp fresh orange juice
3 tbsp water
½ cinnamon stick
8 ripe plum tomatoes, peeled and deseeded
juice of 2 limes
250ml/8fl oz double cream, semi-whipped
125ml/4fl oz yogurt

FOR THE RICOTTA CREAM
zest and juice of 2 oranges
125g/4½oz caster sugar
300g/11oz ricotta cheese
150ml/¼ pint double cream, semi-whipped

sprigs of mint and strands of orange zest, to decorate

SERVES 8

To make the tomato cream, put the sugar, orange juice, water and cinnamon in a pan and boil for 5 minutes. Add the tomatoes, reduce the heat and cook very gently for 1½ hours, until the tomatoes are very soft and slightly candied. Remove the tomatoes from the liquid with a slotted spoon and purée them in a liquidizer with the lime juice. Transfer to a bowl, leave to cool, then fold in the cream and yogurt.

To make the ricotta mixture, put the orange juice and sugar in a pan and bring to the boil, then remove from the heat and leave to cool. Add this mixture to the ricotta and beat well to combine. Stir in the orange zest and fold in the cream.

To serve, put the tomato and ricotta creams in separate piping bags and fill individual glasses with alternate layers. Chill in the fridge for at least an hour, preferably overnight. Decorate with mint and orange zest before serving.

Anita's Rich Chocolate Mousse

This simple yet rich chocolate mousse is a favourite with my family, and makes a regular appearance at dinner parties. Add a dash of mandarin or orange liqueur for a lovely variation.

150g/5oz good-quality plain chocolate
2 eggs, separated
1 tbsp caster sugar
300ml/½ pint double cream, semi-whipped

Break the chocolate into small pieces and melt them in a bowl set over a pan of hot, not boiling, water. Stir until smooth. Add the egg yolks and beat well, then remove from the heat.

Beat the egg whites until they form soft peaks, then add the sugar and continue to beat until the whites are stiff.

Fold the double cream into the chocolate mixture, then finally fold in the egg whites as lightly as possible. Spoon the chocolate mousse into a serving bowl or individual dishes and refrigerate for 4 hours before serving.

133

Cucumber and Mint Granita

Serve this granita as a refreshing palate cleanser between courses or as a first course with a little tomato salad.

50g/2oz caster sugar
200ml/7fl oz water
1 tbsp mint leaves
1kg/2¼lb cucumbers, peeled, deseeded and passed through a juice extractor (see page 146)
1 tbsp lemon juice
a little salt
4 tbsp Greek yogurt
sprigs of mint, to garnish

SERVES 8

Put the sugar and water in a small pan, bring to the boil and simmer until the sugar has dissolved. Add the mint and leave over a low heat for 2–3 minutes to infuse, then strain.

Pour the cucumber juice into a bowl and add the mint-infused liquid, the lemon juice and a little salt. Mix well, then pour into a shallow stainless-steel dish, approximately 30 × 20cm/ 8 × 12 inches and 1–2cm/½–¾ inch deep, and place in the freezer. After 2–3 hours it should be two-thirds set; take it out of the freezer and scrape the mixture with a spoon until it forms loose crystals. Replace in the freezer and repeat once or twice more to attain a tray of loose crystals. The granita should be firm but light in texture. Scoop the granita into glasses, top with a spoonful of Greek yogurt and garnish with sprigs of mint. Serve immediately.

Celery and Lemon Granita

150g/5oz caster sugar
450ml/¾ pint water
10 sprigs of thyme, or lemon thyme if available
10 celery sticks, finely chopped
300ml/½ pint freshly squeezed lemon juice (about 8 lemons)
3 tbsp vodka
celery leaves, to garnish

SERVES 8

Put the sugar and water in a pan, bring to the boil and simmer until the sugar has dissolved. Add the thyme and chopped celery, simmer for 5 minutes then remove from the heat and leave to cool. Stir in the lemon juice and vodka.

Pour the mixture through a fine sieve into a shallow stainless-steel dish, approximately 30 × 20cm/8 × 12 inches and 1–2cm/½–¾ inch deep, and place in the freezer. After 2–3 hours it should be two-thirds set; take it out of the freezer and scrape the mixture with a spoon until it forms loose crystals. Replace in the freezer and repeat once or twice more to attain a tray of loose crystals.

Scoop the granita into glasses, garnish with celery leaves and serve.

WINE NOTES

An Italian Moscato

*C*lockwise from the top: Celery and Lemon Granita, Roasted Tomato Granita (page 136), Fennel Sorbet (page 136), and Cucumber and Mint Granita

135

Roasted Tomato Granita

*This can be served as a light
first course.*

*900g/2lb ripe but firm plum tomatoes,
peeled, cut in half lengthways and
deseeded
2 tbsp extra virgin olive oil
1 small clove garlic, thinly sliced
1 sprig of thyme
200ml/7fl oz water
50g/2oz caster sugar
1 tbsp lemon juice, or to taste
¼ tsp Tabasco sauce
a little salt
sprigs of thyme and basil, to garnish*

SERVES 8

Preheat the oven to 150°C (300°F, Gas Mark 2). Place the tomatoes in a small baking tray or shallow oven-proof dish, brush them with the olive oil and scatter with the garlic and the leaves from the sprig of thyme. Roast in the oven for 1 hour, until they begin to wrinkle and dry but are still plump. Remove and leave to cool.

Bring the water and sugar to the boil in a small pan and stir until the sugar has dissolved. Remove from the heat and leave to cool.

Place the tomatoes and the sugar syrup in a liquidizer and blitz to a purée. Pass the purée through a fine sieve into a bowl, then add the lemon juice, Tabasco sauce and a little salt to taste. Pour into a shallow stainless-steel dish, approximately 30 × 20 cm/8 × 12 inches and 1–2cm/½–¾ inch deep, and place in the freezer. After 2–3 hours it should be two-thirds set; take it out of the freezer and scrape the mixture with a spoon until it forms loose crystals. Replace in the freezer and repeat once or twice more to attain a tray of loose crystals. The granita should be firm but light in texture. Scoop into glasses, garnish with thyme and basil and serve immediately.

Fennel Sorbet

*This goes well with the orange compote
from the Pumpkin and Orange Brûlée
(see page 130), made with a mixture
of citrus fruits.*

*300g/11oz caster sugar
400ml/14fl oz water
600g/1lb 6oz fennel (approximately 3–4
bulbs), roughly chopped
juice of 1 lemon
Pernod, to taste (optional)*

Put the sugar and water in a pan, bring to the boil and simmer until the sugar has dissolved. Add the fennel, reserving some fronds for garnish, and poach gently for 10–15 minutes or until very soft. Pour into a liquidizer and blitz to a fine purée. Strain through a fine sieve and add the lemon juice and some Pernod, if using.

Pour into a sorbetière and freeze until firm, following the manufacturer's instructions. If you don't have a sorbetière, pour the mixture into a bowl and put it in the freezer. After about 30 minutes, when the mixture is beginning to set, remove it from the freezer and beat well with an electric beater or a hand whisk to disperse any ice crystals, then return it to the freezer. Repeat this 2 or 3 times until the sorbet is set firm. Serve garnished with the reserved fronds of fennel.

Cream Cheese Sorbet

500ml/18fl oz milk
175g/6oz caster sugar
zest and juice of 1 small orange
175g/6oz cream cheese

Put the milk, sugar, orange zest and juice in a pan and bring to the boil, then remove from the heat and leave to cool. Stir this mixture into the cream cheese. Pour it into a sorbetière and freeze until firm, following the manufacturer's instructions. If you don't have a sorbetière, pour the mixture into a bowl and put it in the freezer. After about 30 minutes, when the mixture is beginning to set, remove it from the freezer and beat well with an electric beater or hand whisk to disperse any ice crystals, then return it to the freezer. Repeat this 2 or 3 times until the sorbet is set firm.

Lemon Grass Sorbet

250ml/8fl oz freshly squeezed lemon
juice (about 7 lemons)
250ml/8fl oz dry white wine
200g/7oz caster sugar
7 lemon grass stalks

Put all the ingredients in a pan and bring to the boil, then remove from the heat and leave to infuse for 1 hour. Strain through a fine strainer, then pour it into a sorbetière and freeze until firm, following the manufacturer's instructions. If you don't have a sorbetière, pour the mixture into a bowl and put it in the freezer. After about 30 minutes, when the mixture is beginning to set, remove it from the freezer and beat well with an electric beater or hand whisk to disperse any ice crystals, then return it to the freezer. Repeat this 2 or 3 times until the sorbet is set firm.

Black Pepper Ice-Cream

The black pepper gives this ice-cream a subtle spicy flavour. It is particularly good served with marinated orange and grapefruit segments.

9 egg yolks
100g/4oz caster sugar
250ml/8fl oz milk
250ml/8fl oz double cream
1 level tsp freshly ground black pepper

Cream together the egg yolks and half the sugar in a bowl. Put the milk, cream, pepper and remaining sugar in a pan and bring to the boil, then pour it over the egg yolks. Return the mixture to the pan and cook very gently, stirring constantly, until thickened. Strain through a fine strainer and leave to cool, then pour it into an ice-cream maker and freeze until firm, following the manufacturer's instructions. If you don't have an ice-cream maker, pour the mixture into a bowl and put it in the freezer. After about 30 minutes, when it is beginning to set, remove it from the freezer and beat well with an electric beater or hand whisk to disperse any ice crystals, then return it to the freezer. Repeat this 2 or 3 times until it is set firm.

Vegetable and Fruit Larder

The rapidly growing range of fruit and vegetables available has certainly had an interesting impact on our cooking over the last few years. There has been a revolution in choice, and nowadays it is possible to find almost anything with a little patience. Yams, Swiss chard, brightly coloured squashes, papayas and persimmons nestle next to old standbys such as onions, carrots and apples. Sometimes these newcomers are left on the shelf due to uncertainty about how to prepare them. Here is a brief guide to the slightly more unusual fruit and vegetables that appear in this book, as well as some familiar ones that tend to be neglected or misused.

ASPARAGUS

Asparagus is thought to have originated in the Middle East but it is now firmly established in Europe. Regarded as the king of vegetables, it is available throughout the year as an import but the homegrown variety has only a very short season in late spring. Look for crisp, firm stalks, avoiding any that are limp.

Green asparagus is usually grown in the UK, while the French and Italians prefer a fatter white variety. Very fresh local asparagus is a real treat and is best simply steamed and served on its own with a light sauce. Imported green asparagus does not have such a delicate flavour and can be used in mixed vegetable dishes such as stir-fries. The price of imported white asparagus makes it a real luxury item.

To prepare asparagus, trim each spear by snapping off the white woody part. Peel away the outer skin from the base towards the top until the tightly budded tip is reached. How much paring is needed depends on the quality and the freshness of the asparagus. Thin varieties may only need trimming.

BEETROOT

I consider this one of the most underrated of all vegetables. It is usually drenched in vinegar and banished to the salad bowl, where it has no opportunity to show off its sweet, mellow flavour.

Always buy beetroot raw and look for small, firm specimens. Wash them carefully but don't scrub or trim them, as the juices will leach out during cooking if the skin is broken.

When beetroot is young I find it is best simply washed, wrapped in foil, and then baked in a low oven until tender. Older beetroot is better simmered in water. Peel both types after cooking. You will find several recipes for beetroot in this book; try them and experience its versatility.

CELERIAC

This large, knobbly, fragrant root is available throughout the autumn and winter. It has a distinctive celery flavour and is ideal for salads and soups. It has always been more popular in Europe than in the UK.

Choose the smoothest celeriac you can find to avoid wastage when peeling. To prepare, trim the ends, peel off the thick, knobbly skin and use as required. Once peeled it should be used quickly or kept in water acidulated with lemon juice, as it tends to discolour when exposed to the air.

DAIKON RADISH

Also known as mooli, this large, white oriental radish is now widely available all year round. It has a milder flavour than its small red British counterpart. The Japanese use it a great deal, both raw and pickled. It can be shredded and served in salads or added to vegetable stir-fries.

GLOBE ARTICHOKES

These curious members of the thistle family are available throughout the year but are at their best during June and July. Always choose the greenest, firmest, roundest specimens; the leaves should be tightly packed and it should feel heavy for its size.

To prepare a globe artichoke, first snap the stalk off, pulling the tough stem fibres with it. Then you have to be merciless in trimming away all the dark green outer leaves, which are fibrous and inedible, until you reach the tender, yellowish-green inner leaves. With a stainless steel knife, cut off one to two thirds from the top of the artichoke, depending on how pale, and thus tender, the leaves are.

With a paring knife, starting at the stem, trim the base and pare away the remaining tough, dark green outer leaves, rubbing the exposed parts with a squeezed lemon half to prevent discoloration. When the external leaves are removed they will expose the lightly packed central leaves that conceal the hairy choke. Scoop out the raw choke with a teaspoon. Once trimmed, artichokes tend to blacken quickly, so drop them into a large bowl of water acidulated with lemon juice as you prepare them. Some people, myself included, prefer to remove the inner choke when the artichoke has been cooked.

Young green artichokes from France, known as poivrade or pepper artichokes, need hardly any trimming at all, just the removal of some outer leaves to expose the heart.

JAPANESE AUBERGINES
Everyone is familiar nowadays with the long, glossy, dark-purple aubergines that are an essential part of Mediterranean cookery. Less widely known is the small, round Japanese aubergine, which is white or purple and has a sweeter flavour. It doesn't contain the pulpy seeds associated with the larger varieties and does not need salting before use. Otherwise it should be prepared just like any other type of aubergine.

JERUSALEM ARTICHOKES
Jerusalem artichokes are not related to the globe variety, in spite of the similarities in flavour and texture. They were originally brought to Europe from North America and are in fact related to the sunflower. They are at their best from October to February.

To prepare, wash the artichokes, then peel them and cut into even-sized pieces, dropping them in water acidulated with lemon juice to prevent discoloration. Very misshapen ones are easier to peel after parboiling. They can be boiled, steamed or deep-fried, but are especially delicious roasted.

KOHLRABI
This looks rather like a pale green turnip but it is in fact a member of the cabbage family. It is very popular in Germany and Poland but less so in the UK. However, it is now readily available in large supermarkets throughout the winter and is well worth trying. Choose firm, unblemished kohlrabi that are no bigger than a tennis ball. Trim the stalk, and the leaves if they are still attached, then peel them. Boil, steam or braise, as for turnips.

OKRA
These are also known as lady's fingers, due to their long, tapered shape. They are widely used in African, Caribbean and Middle Eastern cookery as well as being an essential ingredient in American gumbos. Okra are now available throughout the year but they are at their best in summer. Always choose the smallest, tenderest ones available as they are generally more digestible; avoid any that look stale and brown.

To prepare, cut off the pointed top and trim lightly to avoid piercing the pod and releasing the central seeds and sticky, gelatinous liquid. Cook them gently in stews or steam or sauté them. Okra has a relatively short shelf life and should not be refrigerated as this causes it to deteriorate even more quickly.

PAPAYA
Papaya, or pawpaw, is shaped like an avocado but has a softer, yellowy-greeny skin and is in fact a large berry. It is ripe when the skin has turned yellow and the stalk end yields slightly when pressed. It cuts open to reveal a salmon-pink interior with black seeds. These are discarded and the flesh is generally eaten raw, although it can be cooked.

PASSION FRUIT
This small, round, purple tropical fruit has a very sweet yet tart flavour. It is now available throughout the year and

is ripe when the skin has wrinkled and the fruit feels heavy. To prepare, simply cut the fruit in half and scoop out the pulpy seeds, which can be eaten as they are or strained for their juice – this is easier if you warm them slightly first. I like to use passion fruit in vinaigrettes and sauces but it can also be experimented with as a marinade ingredient for vegetables such as asparagus.

QUINCE

This was very popular in the past but is quite rare nowadays. It is a rock-hard, yellowy-gold fruit looking rather like a misshapen pear and with patches of grey down. Inedible raw, it is usually steamed or poached and used to make jams and jellies but it is also extremely good combined with apples and pears. Its flesh softens and turns a delicate orangey pink when cooked. Quinces have only a short season in autumn and are not easy to find; try specialist greengrocers and your friends' gardens – many gardens contain an ancient quince tree and the fruit often goes to waste.

SQUASHES

Squashes are generally available all year round but they can be divided into summer and winter varieties. Summer squashes include courgettes and patty pan and are at their best when young and firm. They are completely edible and don't need peeling. As the season progresses, the more robust varieties

such as pumpkin and butternut squash become available. Their skins are inedible and they should be peeled and deseeded before use. Summer squashes generally have a mild, delicate flavour and need only brief cooking, while winter squashes, which are much harder, should be baked, boiled or steamed until tender.

Americans are accustomed to having a huge variety of winter squashes to choose from. These are gradually becoming better known in the UK, and butternut squash in particular is rapidly increasing in popularity. It has a large, bulbous peanut shape and a pleasantly nutty flavour.

SWEET POTATO

There are two main varieties of sweet potatoes: the orange-fleshed one, indigenous to Northern America, and the white-fleshed variety of African and Middle Eastern descent. I prefer the orange one, which has a sweet, chestnutty, almost caramelized flavour. Sweet potatoes are available throughout the autumn and winter. Choose firm, heavy specimens with no soft spots. They can be baked, boiled or mashed, like ordinary potatoes, and in America and the Caribbean they are very popular in desserts.

SWISS CHARD

This underrated vegetable was commonly eaten in Britain in the early part of this century and deserves to have its popularity restored. Chard is

available in the spring and is related to beetroot. It can be considered as two vegetables in one: the leaves, and the long white stalks, or ribs, which are a great delicacy. The leaves have a strong, cabbagey flavour and should be green, firm and crisp; prepare them like spinach or beetroot greens. The stalks have a sweeter, nuttier flavour than beetroot and should be thinly peeled, like celery, to remove the thin, fibrous skin. I like to poach them and serve them simply with melted butter or hollandaise sauce.

TRUFFLES

Truffles are a type of funghi that grow about 30cm/1 foot underground and they are notorious for their fantastically high price. They are the ultimate luxury ingredient, and likely to remain so unless someone manages to devise a way of cultivating them – so far this has proved impossible. They are available in tins or jars but to experience the full power of this astonishingly aromatic fungus you have to splash out and try a fresh truffle. Opinion is divided over which type is best. I prefer the black winter truffle from France, in season from November to March, but the Italian white truffle has its devotees too. Brush fresh truffles thoroughly to remove sand before use. They can be shaved over dishes raw, but if you are lucky enough to have several black truffles they are delicious poached in the oven in Madeira. Truffle oil makes a wonderful addition to salad dressings.

WHITE CHICORY

White chicory, also known as Belgian endive, has a small, spear-shaped head of tightly packed crisp leaves. It is available all year round; look for crisp, pale heads that are heavy for their size. It is usually eaten raw in salads but I prefer to braise it or fry it in butter with a little sugar until slightly caramelized, since it can taste bitter when raw. To prepare, simply trim the root end and remove any discoloured leaves, then separate the leaves or cut the head into rings.

WILD MUSHROOMS

Wild funghi have been appreciated since Roman times, and hunting for mushrooms is a favourite pastime in many European countries. Wild mushrooms are so expensive that it is worth taking time to gather your own. Arm yourself with a handbook to aid identification and don't eat any unless you are absolutely sure they are safe – fatal accidents are not unknown.

Dried mushrooms have a very concentrated flavour, and although they are expensive just a few added to a dish will boost the flavour of cultivated mushrooms no end. They should be soaked in a little warm water for ½–1 hour to reconstitute them; use the soaking liquid in sauces, soups, etc.

Here are some of my favourite mushroom varieties:

Ceps are just as likely to be labelled porcini nowadays, with the renewed interest in Italian cookery. These very superior mushrooms look rather like button mushrooms but have a dark brown skin. They have a very earthy flavour, almost meaty in taste, and are best from May to September. When choosing ceps ensure that they are firm and not worm ridden (as they sometimes can be). Wipe them clean with a damp cloth rather than washing them, since they soak up liquid like a sponge.

Morels are hollow mushrooms with a bizarre, honeycombed appearance and are available in late spring. They are possibly the most expensive of all, with a rich, powerful flavour. They should be washed very thoroughly in water, either whole or cut vertically in half, since they tend to trap sand.

Trompettes de la mort translates as 'horns of death' but these grey, trumpet-shaped mushrooms are also less alarmingly known as horns of plenty. They are delicate and fibrous in texture.

Chanterelles are fragrant, smooth-textured, golden funghi, available from July to December. They tend to trap dirt so they need to be washed very thoroughly several times in cold water, then rinsed and dried in a cloth.

Oyster mushrooms are known in French as *pleurottes*, and it has been said that this name derives from *pleurer* (to cry) – certainly they soak up water all too readily, which is why they should always be wiped with a damp cloth rather than washed. This blue-grey, oyster-shaped mushroom is now available pretty much all year round and has a good flavour.

Shiitake mushrooms have also recently become readily available. Widely used in oriental cookery, they came originally from China and Japan but the ones we buy tend to be imported from Holland. They have firm flesh and a meaty flavour, similar to flat mushrooms. Wipe them with a damp cloth before use.

Vegetarian Pantry

OILS AND SAUCES

Sesame oil is a thick, brown oil extracted from roasted sesame seeds and has a strong flavour. Good for dressings and marinades, it is also occasionally used in small amounts for frying. It needs care, however, as it burns very easily. A milder, lighter-coloured version is also available, made from unroasted seeds.

There is a huge range of **olive oils** available, from France, Italy, Greece, Portugal and other Mediterranean countries. My own preference is for Italian olive oil but it is worth experimenting to find the type you like best. **Extra virgin olive oil** is the least refined and has the strongest, purest flavour; this is what I recommend for the recipes in this book.

Groundnut oil is sometimes known as peanut oil and its mild, unobtrusive flavour is good for use with delicate foods. It can be heated to a very high temperature and hence is particularly suited to frying.

Soy sauce is an essential addition to any storecupboard. This salty condiment is made from fermented soya beans and is usually sold in light or dark varieties. I find light soy sauce much better for general use since it is not as strong and bitter as the dark variety. Also useful is **ketjap manis**, a thick anise-flavoured Indonesian soy sauce made with molasses, spices, herbs and sugar, which give it its characteristic sweet yet piquant taste.

Harissa is a pungent North African relish made from garlic, red chillies, cumin and other spices. It is extremely potent and should be used with caution.

VINEGARS

During the early Eighties when nouvelle cuisine was at its height, vinegars were very much in vogue and even I must confess to having invented my own tea vinegar. Flavours such as raspberry and strawberry were valued for their novelty, but nowadays we have returned to more straightforward varieties. It is well worth buying the best quality available – the flavour of the cheaper vinegars simply isn't as good.

I use good-quality **red wine vinegar** such as Cabernet Sauvignon, available from specialist food stores. **White wine** and **sherry vinegar** are mainly used in sauces and dressings, while **champagne vinegar**, one of my favourites, is ideal for dressings that require a light acidity. **Balsamic vinegar** originated in Italy and is aged in oak barrels for a minimum of ten years and up to 50 years. It has a rich, slightly sweetish taste and is ideal in dressings and marinades. Finally, **rice wine vinegar** is popular in oriental cookery and is very sweet and delicately flavoured. I use it a lot.

GELATINE

Gelatine is made from the hooves and shins of calves, so naturally vegetarians prefer not to use it. Instead, vegetarian equivalents such as gelazone or agar agar, made from seaweed, may be substituted. However, I have never had much success with these products, which tend to have a crumbly texture and lack clarity, so I use gelatine – either granules or the better-quality leaf variety. If you do not want to use gelatine, try one of the substitutes, following the instructions on the packet.

TOFU

This is a soya bean paste that has been pressed into block form. People seem to love or hate it and it has a rather poor image as a bland mainstay of old-style vegetarian food. Certainly it isn't always used as imaginatively as it could be. Tofu can be fried or grilled but it is best to marinate it first with something piquant, such as horseradish, garlic or fresh herbs. I prefer the firmer type to silken tofu.

SOYA MILK

This milky liquid made from the versatile soya bean is a useful alternative for people who have allergies to cow's milk. I like to use it occasionally for its earthy flavour.

CHEESES

Goat's cheese has become very popular over the last ten years and many new varieties have been developed, ranging from mild, soft, fresh cheeses to firm, pungent logs. I particularly favour the French crottin de Chavignol and the English Golden Cross.

Ricotta is an unripened Italian cheese made from cow's milk whey. Its mild flavour makes it suitable for both sweet and savoury dishes. If possible, avoid the ricotta sold in tubs, which is almost completely characterless. Instead buy it loose from a good delicatessen and eat it when it is very fresh, otherwise the sweet, milky flavour becomes slightly tainted.

The very best **mozzarella** is made from buffalo's milk but the cheaper cow's milk variety is acceptable in most recipes. The important thing is to buy mozzarella packed in water. It is readily available like this, sold in little plastic bags, and simply needs draining before use.

Mascarpone is an extremely rich cream cheese which probably owes its recent popularity to the fact that it is an essential ingredient in one of Italy's most famous desserts – tiramisu. However, I prefer to use it in savoury dishes and sauces. It has a sweetish, fairly neutral flavour.

Parmesan is the king of Italian cheeses. There are many types available, including some second-class varieties such as grana Padano, but by far the best is Parmigiano reggiano. Quality does not come cheap and reggiano is very expensive, but well worth it. Always buy Parmesan in a piece and grate it freshly yourself. A well-wrapped chunk will keep for ages and the flavour is incomparably better than the ready-grated Parmesan available in packets.

Gorgonzola is considered by many to be one of the world's greatest cheeses. Made in Lombardy, it has a creamy texture which is given piquancy by the blue veins running through it. I use it a lot in sauces and salad dressings.

Gruyère is a hard Swiss cheese with a sweet, nutty flavour that lends itself well to sauces and gratins. It is an essential ingredient of that Swiss speciality, fondue.

GRAINS AND PULSES

The most fragrant and flavoursome of rices is **basmati**, which has a delicate, almost nutty flavour. It grows in the foothills of the Himalayas and usually accompanies savoury dishes such as curries or is used to make pilaffs.

To make Italian risottos you need proper **Italian risotto rice**. The most popular variety is Arborio, a short grain rice which is very starchy and can absorb large amounts of liquid. Other risotto rices include **Carnaroli** and **Vialome Nano**.

Wild rice is not in fact a rice grain at all but the seed of a wild grass, harvested by canoe from the rivers of Minnesota and Canada. It is a very expensive commodity but its heavy, smoky flavour is worth the price. Soak wild rice overnight to cut down the cooking time, then cook as for any other rice.

Pearl barley is the most commonly available type of barley and is mildly flavoured and chewy. Its outer husk has been removed, making it slightly less nutritious than whole barley but quicker cooking. Cook it in plenty of boiling salted water and use in broths, thick soups and casseroles. Less well known is **millet**, a small, round grain with a flavour rather like cornmeal. I use it to make pilaffs or as a substitute for couscous.

Polenta is a coarsely ground corn meal from Italy, where it is mixed with boiling water and cooked slowly to make a thick, porridgey stew. This can be served as it is or poured out on to a board and left to set, then cut into pieces and grilled or fried. There is now a quick-cooking variety available which is ready in about 5–10 minutes and saves on 40 minutes' stirring, but I find nothing beats the traditional slow-cooking polenta for flavour and texture.

Bulgar wheat, or cracked wheat, is popular in Middle Eastern dishes such as tabbouleh. It can be simply soaked in water until swollen and fluffy or simmered to make a pilaff.

Couscous looks like a grain but is really a type of tiny pasta made from semolina. It should be soaked before cooking, when it fluffs up and doubles in size. However, you are more likely to find a partially cooked version for sale nowadays, which, like bulgar wheat, only needs soaking in hot water to make it swell and soften. Couscous is usually served in Morocco with a spicy stew of meat, fish or vegetables, also known as couscous.

Matzoh meal is a staple of Jewish cookery, and is made from wheat to which water has been added to produce a creamy, white, polenta-like powder. It is traditionally used to make unleavened bread, to coat food for frying or to bind ingredients together, but I use it like polenta occasionally.

Of all the many different types of pulses there are a few that I use regularly. **Chick peas** are good for soups, sauces and dips. They are especially popular in Middle Eastern dishes – hummus, for example – but are also a mainstay of Spanish cooking. In India they are ground into flour for making bread. Dried chick peas make a good storecupboard staple, while the canned ones which just need heating through, are also useful to keep in stock.

Black beans, also known as turtle beans, are used extensively in Central and South American cookery. They have only recently become widely avaiiable in the UK and are worth trying for their distinctive flavour and the thick black sauce they produce during cooking.

Puy lentils, a small, French, blueish-brown pulse, are much prized for their meaty flavour and because they keep their shape well when cooked, making them suitable for salads as well as soups and stews.

DRIED SPICES

For me, one of the pleasures of cooking is experimenting with herbs and spices from all over the world. Now that most of them are readily available, they open up a wealth of flavours and ideas for the home cook.

Here are some of my favourites:

Caraway seeds are very popular in Eastern Europe and Scandinavia, where they are added not only to savoury dishes such as sauerkraut, dumplings and goulash but also to breads, biscuits, cakes and liqueurs. They have a warm, aromatic, slightly aniseedy flavour. Label them carefully, since they look very like cumin seeds.

Cardamom are small aromatic pods containing black seeds, used as a fragrant spice to perfume Asian dishes. Although ground cardamom is available it quickly loses its flavour.

Cinnamon, one of the world's oldest spices, has been popular in Britain for centuries. The bark of a small tree, cinnamon is available in 'quills' or powdered, and should be used sparingly.

Chinese five-spice powder is a blend of dried spices used as a basic flavouring in Chinese cooking. There are many different varieties, and the most popular combination consists of star anise, cassia (a cinamon-flavoured spice), anise pepper, cloves and fennel seed.

Coriander is a dual-purpose spice: the mild, slightly citrussy seeds are used as a spice in marinades, sauces, etc., while the fresh leaf is a pungent herb known variously as **green coriander, Chinese parsley** or **cilantro.**

Cumin is a powerfully flavoured seed, popular in Asian and Middle Eastern cookery and used mainly in highly spiced dishes such as chutneys, sauces, stews, etc. Use it with caution, as it can overwhelm other flavours.

Curry powder is a packaged powdered spice mix essentially sold as a convenience product. There is no substitute for blending your own spices to make curry powder and if you try my blend on page 154 you will see just how easy it is to prepare – and what a difference it makes to the finished dish.

Fennel, like coriander, is both a herb and a spice. The feathery tops of the fennel bulb are very good with fish, while the anise-flavoured seeds can be used to add fragrance to both sweet and savoury dishes.

Fenugreek is a small, rib-shaped spice with a strong, bitter-sweet flavour. It is used extensively in Asian cookery, especially in curries.

Saffron is the world's most expensive spice. Its bright yellowy-orange strands are the stamens of the crocus plant and they add both flavour and colour to dishes. A cheaper powdered form is available but its flavour cannot be compared to that of fresh saffron.

Star anise is a star-shaped spice widely used in oriental cooking and is one of the components of the popular Chinese five-spice powder. It adds a pleasant aniseed flavour to dishes.

Turmeric is a member of the ginger family and resembles ginger root in appearance. It is most commonly available as a vivid yellow powder and is used in Asian cooking to add both colour and flavour.

Vanilla pods are the fruit of an orchid plant indigenous to South America. These long black pods are very fragrant and should be split open to extract the tiny black seeds. Vanilla is very expensive and many people use vanilla essence instead, a synthetic concoction that is no substitute at all for the real thing. Vanilla extract is better, since it is made from pure vanilla, but generally for the best flavour you need to use pods. After a vanilla pod has been used to flavour a sauce it can be rinsed and dried, then placed in a jar of caster sugar to make vanilla sugar.

FRESH SPICES

Ginger root is now readily available fresh, and for me it is one of life's greatest treasures. Far superior in flavour to dried ginger it simply needs peeling before use. It keeps very well in the refrigerator.

Lemon grass is a fragrant, lemony plant used extensively in Southeast Asian cooking and is now available in most large supermarkets. It should be chopped or bruised before use to bring out the flavour. Try adding lemon grass to soups, sauces, salad dressings – anything where you want a delicate oriental flavour.

Fresh chillies are grown all over the world and range in potency from mild to throat-searingly hot, such as the Mexican habanero. Usually the larger the chilli the milder the flavour, but this isn't always the case. Recent research has shown that the heat in the chilli may be contained not in the seeds, as was previously thought, but in the white channel that holds the seeds. Whatever the theory, one thing is sure: you need to wear rubber gloves when handling chillies to prevent them burning your hands – or, worse, affecting your eyes if you accidentally rub them after contact with chillies. **Dried chilli flakes** and **powdered chillies** are available and both make an acceptable substitute.

Useful Equipment

Always buy the best-quality equipment you can afford and think of it as a long-term investment. A well-stocked and well-maintained kitchen helps no end in the production of good food. Here is a guide to what I believe every kitchen should have.

PANS

Good-quality **saucepans and frying pans** are essential to good cooking, so never economize on them. If you choose heavy-based stainless steel or cast iron and look after them well they should last you a lifetime. A good selection of different sizes is invaluable so that you can use the correct-size pan for the job in hand.

KNIVES

The **best knives** are made from stainless steel. They are expensive, but buying cheaply produced knives is a false economy. Well-made knives, kept sharp and clean, will last for many years and more than repay their cost.

USEFUL GADGETS

There are so many little gadgets on the market that it is easy to get carried away and end up spending a lot of money on items you will hardly ever use. For me, these are the essentials: a good set of reliable kitchen scales; rubber spatulas, wooden spoons and stainless steel slotted draining spoons; supple, stainless steel whisks in several sizes; colanders, sieves and fine conical strainers (chinois), varying in mesh size; ladles made in one piece from stainless steel; pastry cutters, measuring jugs and a good pepper mill.

Although not essential, a **marble slab and rolling pin** are best for pastry. A **mandoline** is ideal for slicing vegetables very finely and evenly. A **salad spinner** can be bought very cheaply and will ensure perfectly dry leaves for green salads.

DISHES AND TINS

Several of the recipes in this book call for **ramekin or soufflé dishes**. It's worth having a selection of these straight-sided china dishes in different sizes, plus a range of ovenproof baking dishes, including earthenware gratin dishes. Try to build up a collection of baking tins, too, including small items such as tartlet moulds and individual metal baking rings, plus loose-bottomed tart tins and several baking sheets (cast iron is best for these as it does not buckle). They will all prove invaluable as you expand your repertoire.

ELECTRICAL EQUIPMENT

There are a few items of electrical equipment that have become indispensable. A **centrifugal juice extractor** may seem like a luxury but I find it invaluable. There are several models available and some are now very reasonably priced. It should be a standard piece of equipment in the domestic kitchen, alongside the food processor. Its versatility is astounding, as freshly squeezed vegetable and herb juices can form the basis of so many dishes, including sauces and mayonnaise, giving them an unparalleled freshness and intensity of flavour. Throughout this book you will find recipes that call for a juice extractor but if you don't have one you can purée the ingredient in a liquidizer and then strain the juices through a fine sieve or a piece of muslin. If you are puréeing herbs in this way you will need to add a little water: simply wash them and put them in the machine without draining.

These days, most dedicated cooks possess a **liquidizer**. It takes a lot of the hard work out of puréeing soups and sauces. An **electric mixer** is useful for a variety of tasks, such as beating, whisking and even kneading bread dough, while an **electric hand beater** is very good for sabayons or for finishing off soups where you want a light, frothy consistency. A **food**

processor makes life in the kitchen a lot easier and you will find it invaluable for many of the recipes in this book.

There are several brands of hand-operated and electric **pasta machines** now available, with a range of attachments for making every type of pasta, from lasagne to tagliatelle to ravioli. They are easy to use and can be fun as well as rewarding. It's worth shopping around, as prices vary a lot.

A **sorbetière**, or ice-cream maker, can be expensive, but it is well worth investing in a good-quality model to make really fine-textured sorbets and ice-creams. It opens up a wealth of possibilities for the home cook.

I like to use a **spice or coffee grinder** to prepare spice mixtures such as Home-made Curry Powder (see page 154). The fragrance given off from freshly pulverized spices far outweighs the convenience of using ready-ground versions.

Basic Recipes

Vegetable Stock

There are many myths about making stock – that it is time-consuming, difficult, etc. However, this stock can be put together very quickly and will keep for up to 5 days in the fridge or 1 month in the freezer.

Some good vegetable stock cubes are now available but there are still far too many using herbs as the staple ingredients. It is well worth experimenting with different brands until you find one you like.

2 tbsp extra virgin olive oil
1 onion, roughly chopped
1 small leek, roughly chopped
75g/3oz celeriac, roughly chopped
2 large carrots, roughly chopped
1 celery stick, roughly chopped
75g/3oz white cabbage, roughly chopped
½ head fennel, roughly chopped
4 cloves garlic, chopped
125ml/4fl oz white wine (optional)
4 black peppercorns
1 sprig of thyme
1 small bay leaf
1.5 litres/2½ pints water
2 tsp sea salt

MAKES ABOUT 1 LITRE/1¾ PINTS

Heat the olive oil in a large saucepan, add all the vegetables and cook gently for about 5 minutes until softened.

Add the wine if using, then add the peppercorns, thyme, bay leaf and water. Bring to the boil, add the sea salt and cook for 40 minutes or until reduced by a third of its original volume.

Pour the stock through a fine strainer and leave to cool. Keep in the refrigerator until required.

Dark Vegetable Stock

4 tbsp vegetable oil
½ onion, roughly chopped
150g/5oz carrots, roughly chopped
50g/2oz leeks, roughly chopped
50g/2oz celery, roughly chopped
2 cloves garlic, chopped
100g/4oz flat mushrooms
* roughly chopped*
2 ripe beef tomatoes, roughly chopped
2 sprigs of thyme
a few parsley stalks
1 bay leaf
1 heaped tsp sugar
1.5 litres/2½ pints water
½ tbsp sea salt
2 tbsp dark soy sauce

MAKES ABOUT 1 LITRE/1¾ PINTS

Heat the oil in a heavy-based pan, add the onion, carrots, leeks, celery and garlic and cook for 5 minutes, until lightly coloured. Add the mushrooms

and sauté for another 5 minutes over a low heat, until golden. Add the tomatoes, herbs and sugar and cook for 5 minutes then add the water. Bring to the boil, add the sea salt and skim off any impurities that rise to the surface. Reduce the heat and simmer for 45 minutes.

Stir in the soy sauce, strain the stock through a fine strainer and leave to cool. Keep in the refrigerator until required.

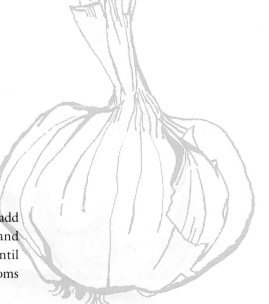

*B*rown Mushroom Stock

An ideal stock for mushroom-based and earthy vegetable dishes.

50g/2oz unsalted butter
3 shallots, finely sliced
1 clove garlic, sliced
600g/1lb 6 oz button mushrooms,
  roughly chopped
300g/11oz flat mushrooms,
  roughly chopped
½ tbsp tomato purée
2 ripe tomatoes, roughly chopped
1 litre/1¾ pints water
a few parsley stalks

MAKES ABOUT 600ML/1 PINT

Melt the butter in a large saucepan, add the shallots and garlic and sweat until softened; do not let them brown. Add the mushrooms and cook, stirring well, until they are deep brown and slightly caramelized.

Add the tomato purée and the tomatoes and cook for 10 minutes, then add the water and parsley stalks and bring to the boil. Skim well to remove any impurities, then reduce the heat and simmer for 20–25 minutes. Strain the stock through a fine strainer and leave to cool. Keep in the refrigerator until required.

*C*hicken Stock

1.5kg/3½lb chicken bones
2 carrots, chopped
2 celery sticks, chopped
1 large leek, chopped
2 onion cloutes (see page 149)
1 bay leaf
2 sprigs of thyme

MAKES ABOUT 1 LITRE/1¾ PINTS

Place the bones in a deep saucepan, cover with cold water and bring slowly to the boil, skimming off any impurities that rise to the surface. Add the vegetables and herbs to the pan, reduce the heat and simmer gently for 4 hours. Strain the stock through a fine sieve and leave to cool. Keep in the refrigerator until required

*B*asic White Sauce

The addition of mustard gives extra body to this sauce. Use it as a base for gratins, or add mushrooms, herbs, etc., to complement the flavours of the dish you plan to serve it with. Replace the milk with well-flavoured stock if you like.

300ml/½ pint milk
½ onion cloute (see note below)
15g/½oz unsalted butter
15g/½oz plain flour
½ tsp Dijon mustard
salt and freshly ground black pepper

MAKES 300ML/½ PINT

Put the milk and onion cloute in a pan, bring to the boil, then remove from the heat and leave to stand for 5 minutes. Melt the butter in a separate pan and add the flour to make a roux. Cook gently, stirring, for 2–3 minutes.

Remove the onion from the milk and add the milk to the roux a little at a time, stirring constantly. Bring slowly to the boil, then reduce the heat and cook very gently for 20–25 minutes, stirring occasionally.

Finally, add the mustard, season to taste and strain through a fine sieve.

Note: An onion cloute is an onion studded with 3–4 cloves, used to flavour milk in basic sauces such as this one.

VARIATIONS
CHEESE SAUCE
Stir into the finished sauce 75g/3oz grated or crumbled cheese, such as goat's cheese, Cheddar, Stilton, etc.

RICH WHITE SAUCE
For a richer, silkier sauce, stir in 3 tablespoons of double cream.

White Butter Sauce

Also known as **beurre blanc,** *this classic sauce may seem a little daunting at first. Have faith; if you follow the recipe exactly it is quick, easy and a good base for many variations. A useful safety measure for the nervous cook is to add 2 tablespoons of double cream to the shallot reduction. This acts as a stabilizer and the sauce is less likely to separate.*

2 large shallots, finely chopped
4 tbsp dry white wine
3 tbsp white wine vinegar or
   champagne vinegar
200g/7oz chilled unsalted butter, cut
   into small pieces

MAKES ABOUT 150ML/¼ PINT

Place the shallots, wine and vinegar in a heavy-based pan and bring to the boil. Reduce the heat and simmer until the liquid is reduced by just over two-thirds of its original volume. Remove the pan from the heat and cool slightly.

   Put the pan over a very gentle heat and add the butter a piece at a time, whisking vigorously until all the butter is used up and the sauce is thick and shiny. Strain through a fine strainer and serve immediately, or keep it warm for up to an hour (see Hollandaise Sauce, page 151). If the sauce is too thick, add a little water: it should be the right consistency to cling to the back of a spoon.

VARIATIONS
HERB BUTTER SAUCE
Add 2 tablespoons of chopped fresh herbs, such as tarragon, dill, basil, etc.

WATERCRESS SAUCE
Pass a bunch of fresh watercress through a juice extractor (see page 146) and add the juice to the sauce.

LEMON BUTTER SAUCE
Add the zest and juice of 1 lemon.

White Butter Fondue

This sauce forms a neutral base to which flavouring ingredients such as herbs may be added. By replacing the stock with fresh vegetable juices such as celery, pepper, asparagus or carrot, you can make a delicious, fresh-tasting vegetable sauce.

125ml/4fl oz vegetable stock (see
   page 148) or water
125g/4½oz chilled unsalted butter, cut
   into small pieces
a little lemon juice
salt and freshly ground black pepper

MAKES ABOUT 150ML/¼ PINT

Bring the stock or water to the boil in a small pan, reduce the heat and cool slightly. Then whisk in the butter pieces a few at a time to form an emulsion. Finally stir in the lemon juice, salt and pepper.

*H*ollandaise Sauce

One of the problems with emulsified sauces such as this one and the previous two is keeping them hot, as they have a tendency to split or curdle. However, I find that they keep very well for up to an hour in a vacuum flask.

If the Hollandaise sauce should curdle while you are making it, it can be rescued by whisking in a little boiling water or by putting another egg yolk into a clean pan and gradually whisking in the curdled sauce.

1 shallot, chopped
3 tbsp white wine vinegar
8 white peppercorns, coarsely crushed
3 egg yolks
225g/8oz butter, clarified (see note below)
salt and freshly ground black pepper
cayenne pepper, to taste
juice of ½ lemon, or to taste

MAKES ABOUT 300ML/½ PINT

Put the shallot, white wine vinegar and crushed peppercorns into a pan and bring to the boil. Remove from the heat, add the egg yolks and 2 tablespoons of water, then transfer the mixture to a bowl set over a pan of hot water. Whisk with a balloon whisk until it thickens and becomes opaque, about 3–4 minutes. Then gradually whisk in the still-warm clarified butter to form an emulsion. Season the sauce with salt, pepper, cayenne and lemon juice to taste.

Note: To clarify butter, place 225g/8oz unsalted butter in a small deep pan and heat gently until it begins to boil. Boil for 2 minutes, then carefully filter the butter through a fine conical strainer, leaving the white milky sediment in the pan. The resulting clarified butter can be used in many ways; particularly for frying, since it can be heated to high temperatures without burning.

VARIATIONS
BEARNAISE SAUCE
Add 1 tablespoon of chopped fresh herbs, such as tarragon, parsley, basil and chervil.

AUBERGINE SAUCE
Cook a diced aubergine in a little olive oil until soft, purée it in a food processor and pass through a fine sieve. Stir 5 tablespoons of the purée into the sauce with ½ teaspoon of chopped basil.

*V*anilla Custard Sauce

175ml/6fl oz milk
175ml/6fl oz double cream
1 vanilla pod, split
4 egg yolks
75g/3oz caster sugar

MAKES ABOUT 450ML/¾ PINT

Put the milk, cream and vanilla pod into a saucepan and bring slowly to the boil. Remove from the heat and leave to infuse for a few minutes, then take out the vanilla pod.

Beat the egg yolks with the sugar until well creamed, then stir in the warm milk mixture. Return to the heat and cook very gently, stirring, until the sauce is thick enough to coat the back of the spoon. Don't let it come anywhere near boiling or it will curdle.

*T*omato Concassée

I use this as a base for many vegetarian dishes and vary the herbs according to the dish I plan to use it in.

2 tbsp extra virgin olive oil
25g/1oz unsalted butter
2 shallots, finely chopped
2 cloves garlic, crushed
900g/2lb firm ripe tomatoes, peeled, deseeded and finely chopped
2 tsp tomato purée
1 tbsp tomato ketchup
½ bay leaf
1–2 sprigs of thyme
a pinch of celery salt
salt and freshly ground black pepper

MAKES ABOUT 300ML/½ PINT

Heat the oil and butter in a pan, add the shallots and garlic and cook over a gentle heat until lightly coloured. Add the tomatoes, the purée and the ketchup, then stir in the herbs and a little seasoning and cook over a gentle heat for 10–15 minutes, until thick and chunky. Add a little celery salt and adjust the seasoning to taste. For a smoother sauce, strain through a fine strainer.

Grilled Tomato Sauce

This is my variation on the grilled tomato sauce prepared at the famous Greens vegetarian restaurant in San Francisco. The grilled tomatoes impart a light smoky flavour. You can make a red pepper sauce in the same way.

900g/2lb ripe tomatoes
salt and freshly ground black pepper
5 tbsp extra virgin olive oil
½ onion, roughly chopped
2 cloves garlic, crushed
a little fresh or dried thyme
a little fresh or dried oregano
1 tsp tomato purée
a pinch of sugar
90ml/3fl oz tomato juice (optional)
250ml/8fl oz vegetable or chicken stock
  (see pages 148-9)

MAKES ABOUT 300ML/½ PINT

Cut the tomatoes in half horizontally and remove the seeds. Place them on a baking sheet, sprinkle with a little salt and 2 tablespoons of the olive oil, then place them under a hot grill for 8–10 minutes until charred.

Meanwhile, heat the remaining oil in a pan, add the onion, garlic and herbs and sweat until translucent. Add the grilled tomatoes and tomato purée and cook for 3–4 minutes. Add the sugar, the tomato juice if using, and a little seasoning, then pour in the stock and bring to the boil, stirring occasionally. Reduce the heat and simmer for 12–15 minutes, then adjust the seasoning and pass through a fine strainer.

SPICY TOMATO SAUCE
Replace the olive oil with chilli oil, or just add 2 chopped small red chillies to the above recipe.

Genoese Pesto Sauce

Possibly the most popular sauce in Italian cookery. Try making orange pesto by adding the juice of 1 orange and 1 teaspoon of finely grated orange zest. This is excellent with leeks or asparagus.

75g/3oz basil leaves
2 cloves garlic, peeled
1 tbsp pine kernels
2 tbsp finely grated Parmesan cheese
salt and freshly ground black pepper
a pinch of sugar
100ml/3½fl oz extra virgin olive oil

MAKES ABOUT 150ML/¼ PINT

Put all the ingredients except the oil in a liquidizer or food processor and blitz until very finely chopped. Slowly add the oil while the motor is still running, until the pesto is almost smooth and has a grainy, slightly runny texture. Adjust the seasoning to taste.

Rocket Pesto

This unusual pesto makes a very good accompaniment to pasta dishes and stuffed vegetables.

100g/4oz rocket leaves
2 cloves garlic, peeled
15g/½oz pine kernels
125ml/4fl oz extra virgin olive oil
1 tbsp freshly grated Parmesan cheese
a little lemon juice
a pinch of sugar
salt and freshly ground pepper

MAKES ABOUT 300ML/½ PINT

Place the rocket and garlic in a blender or food processor (or more traditionally a mortar) and process together. Add the pine kernels, then while the motor is running pour in the olive oil little by little to form an emulsion. Finally, add the Parmesan, lemon juice, sugar and seasoning and process until almost smooth but still slightly grainy in texture. Adjust the seasoning to taste.

Black Olive Tapenade

125g/4½oz black olives, stoned
15g/½oz capers
2 cloves garlic, crushed
4 tbsp olive oil
salt and freshly ground black pepper

MAKES ABOUT 175G/6OZ

Chop the olives and capers very finely, mix with the garlic and olive oil and season to taste; alternatively blitz everything together in a food processor. Store in the refrigerator.

Tomato Tapenade

75g/3oz Oven-dried Tomatoes (see right) or sun-dried tomatoes
25g/1oz capers
25g/1oz green olives, stoned
2 cloves garlic, crushed
1 tsp rosemary
1 tsp lemon juice
2 tbsp olive oil
salt and freshly ground black pepper

MAKES ABOUT 175G/6OZ

Prepare this in the same way as for Black Olive Tapenade (above).

Oven-dried Tomatoes

This way of drying tomatoes really accentuates their flavour and is more subtle than sun-dried tomatoes. If you preserve them in oil they are excellent served with some freshly chopped parsley and green olives. I also like to keep the tomato skins as whole as possible when peeling them, then place them alongside the tomatoes in the oven to dry. The resulting crisp skin is delicate in flavour and adds a little crunchiness to a garnish.

MAKES ABOUT 150G/5OZ

2 tbsp extra virgin olive oil
12 plum tomatoes, peeled and halved lengthways
salt and freshly ground black pepper
1 level tsp caster sugar
6 basil leaves, roughly chopped
2 sprigs of thyme
4 cloves garlic, finely chopped

Brush a small baking dish with a little of the olive oil and place the tomatoes in it. Season them with salt, pepper and the sugar, then sprinkle them liberally with the herbs and garlic. Brush with the remaining olive oil and place in the oven on the lowest possible setting for about 4 hours – or even overnight – until most of the moisture has gone.

To keep the oven-dried tomatoes, store them in a jar with some slivers of fresh garlic and basil leaves and top up with olive oil.

Gribiche Sauce

This is good with steamed or baked potatoes or poached artichokes.

1 quantity of Basic Mayonnaise (see page 52)
2 tsp chopped gherkins
1 tbsp chopped cocktail capers
1 tsp chopped tarragon
1 tsp chopped chervil
1 egg, hard-boiled and finely chopped

MAKES ABOUT 300ML/½ PINT

Put the mayonnaise into a bowl and mix in all the remaining ingredients.

Raita

This is usually made with cucumber but I prefer it without.

125ml/4fl oz yogurt
15 mint leaves, finely chopped
1 tsp ground cumin
1 red chilli, deseeded and very finely chopped
2 tsp lemon juice
1 tbsp extra virgin olive oil
salt and freshly ground black pepper

MAKES ABOUT 150ML/¼ PINT

Mix all the ingredients together in a bowl. Serve the Raita with curries, as a dip for vegetable tempura or as a salad dressing.

Asian Dipping Sauce

During my early years training to be a chef I was fortunate enough to work in small Chinese and Indian restaurants, where I developed a liking for Eastern spices and flavourings. This dipping sauce is one of my favourites; light and delicate, it is typical of the clean flavours prevalent in Chinese cookery. It can be used as a dip for vegetable fritters and as a marinade for vegetable salads.

1 tbsp light soy sauce
2 shallots, finely chopped
2 tbsp rice wine vinegar
2 tsp sesame oil
½ tbsp caster sugar
½ tbsp finely grated fresh ginger root
½ small red chilli, deseeded and
  finely chopped

Mix all the ingredients together in a bowl, cover and keep in the refrigerator until needed.

Piquant Lemon Relish

Preserved lemons have long been a feature of Indian cookery, prepared with mustard seeds, coriander, chilli, etc. This recipe is not so spicy and is fragrant with herbs.

6 lemons, cut into 5mm/¼ inch slices
75g/3oz caster sugar
1 tbsp sea salt or kosher salt
2 bay leaves, broken up
1 tbsp oregano
2 dried chillies, finely chopped
olive oil

MAKES ENOUGH TO FILL A 900G/
2LB JAR

Blanch the lemon slices in boiling water for 2 minutes, drain them in a colander and dry in a cloth. Lay out half the slices in a shallow dish. Mix the sugar and salt together and sprinkle them over the lemons, then arrange the remaining lemons on top and sprinkle over the remaining sugar and salt. Leave to marinate in the refrigerator for 36 hours.

Remove the lemons and arrange them in layers in a glass preserving jar, adding the herbs and chillies between the layers. Pour in olive oil to cover, making sure that all the ingredients are submerged. Close the jar tightly and store in the refrigerator for up to 3 weeks. Chop the lemons up quite finely before use, like a pickle.

Home-made Curry Powder

There are many different brands of curry powder now available but none can compare with the home-made variety.

This recipe, which I acquired during my trips to the Caribbean Islands, is well worth the effort. Do not make too much at once; for best results prepare only what you need.

1 tsp cardamom pods, crushed
2 tsp cumin seeds
2 tsp black mustard seeds
2 tsp black peppercorns
2 tsp fenugreek
3 tbsp coriander seeds
2 tsp aniseed
4 tsp ground turmeric
½ tsp ground cinnamon

Preheat the oven to 180°C (350°F, Gas Mark 4). Heat an ovenproof frying pan over a medium heat. Add the first 7 ingredients and then transfer to the oven to dry-roast for 3–4 minutes, until they become fragrant. Leave the spices to cool before grinding them to a fine powder in a liquidizer or a coffee grinder. Stir in the ground turmeric and cinnamon, then transfer the mixture to a sealed glass jar. Store in a dry place and use as required.

Basic Shortcrust Pastry

250g/9oz plain flour, sifted
175g/6oz chilled unsalted butter, cut
  into small cubes
1 egg, beaten
a pinch of salt

Put the sifted flour on a work surface or in a large bowl. Add the diced butter and blend together with your fingertips until it has a soft, sandy texture. Make a well in the centre and add the beaten egg and salt. Gently mix together with your fingertips to form a smooth, even dough.

Cover in cling film and refrigerate for up to 30 minutes or until required.

VARIATIONS
CHEESE PASTRY
Add 3 tablespoons of freshly grated Parmesan cheese with the butter.

HERB PASTRY
Add 2 tablespoons of chopped herbs, such as parsley, thyme or tarragon, with the butter.

ALMOND PASTRY
Add 25g/1oz ground almonds with the butter.

Basic Sweet Pastry

This sweet pastry is very rich and is ideal for fruit tarts.

325g/12oz plain flour, sifted
225g/8oz unsalted butter, cut into small
  pieces (at room temperature)
a pinch of salt
100g/4oz icing sugar, sifted
finely grated zest of ½ lemon
1 egg

Put the sifted flour on a work surface and make a well in the centre. Put the butter, salt, sugar and lemon zest in the well and then add the egg. With your fingertips, gradually bring the flour into the centre until all the ingredients come together to form a soft dough. Knead lightly for 1 minute until completely smooth, then form the dough into a ball, place in a bowl and cover with cling film. Leave to rest in the fridge for 2 hours.

Mashed Potato Pastry

325g/12oz potatoes
125g/4½oz softened unsalted butter
250g/9oz plain flour, sifted
a pinch of salt

Cook the potatoes in boiling salted water until tender, then drain well and pass through a sieve to make a fairly dry purée – you should end up with 250g/9oz purée, to give equal weights of flour and potato. Beat the butter into the potato purée, then fold in the flour and salt and work to a pliable dough. Leave to rest in the fridge for up to 1 hour before using.

Index